Rabindranath
TAGORE

GLEANINGS OF THE ROAD

Translated from the Bengali original *Pather Sanchoy* by
Somdatta Mandal

THORNBIRD
NIYOGI BOOKS

Published by
NIYOGI BOOKS
Block D, Building No. 77,
Okhla Industrial Area, Phase-I,
New Delhi-110 020, INDIA
Tel: 91-11-26816301, 26818960
Email: niyogibooks@gmail.com
Website: www.niyogibooksindia.com

Design: Nabanita Das

ISBN: 978-93-86906-25-0
Publication: 2018

Printed at: Niyogi Offset Pvt. Ltd., New Delhi, India

Contents

Englander Bhabuksamaj
The Thoughtful Society of England

Englander Palligram O Padri
The English Village and the Clergy

Sangeet
Music

Samajbhed
Social Difference

Seemar Sarthakata
Justification of Limits

Seema O Asimata
Limit and Infinity

Sikshabidhi
The Methods of Education

Lakshya O Siksha
Aims and Education

Americar Chithi
Letter from America

Bichitra/ Bilat-Jatrir Patra
Letter from a Traveller to Vilayet

Seven Letters

Introduction

I

Rabindranath Tagore was an itinerant traveller. He had the opportunity to travel with his family members from his childhood days. His grandfather, Dwarakanath Tagore, was the second person among educated Indians (after Raja Ram Mohan Roy) to sail to England. Thus it is no wonder that the lust for distance pulled him out of home and hearth repeatedly, throughout his life. On September 20, 1878 he accompanied his brother Satyendranath and sailed for England for the first time. We get his experiences of travelling in a ship and glimpses of his trip from the letters he wrote home and which were published serially in the family periodical *Bharati* (between *Baisakh* 1286 B.S. and *Sravana* 1287 B.S.). In 1881, these letters were published under the title *Yurop Probashir Patra* [Letters from a Sojourner in Europe].

In 1904, these letters were again included in the Hitabadi edition of Tagore's *Granthabali*. Later, Rabindranath, embarrassed by his juvenile bravado, edited his letters before including them in his book *Paschatya Bhraman* in 1936. This volume included both *Yurop Probashir Patra* and *Yurop Jatrir*

Diary. He also included a Preface in the form of a letter(August 29, 1936) to Charuchandra Dutta, the retired ICS officer who spent his time in Santiniketan from 1931 to 1938, in which he states, 'I would like this book to be regarded as a work of literature and not history.' He further wrote, 'I did not go as a wayfarer when I first travelled to England in my early years. What I meant to say is that my vision was not restricted to seeing everything fleetingly as I walked along the road. I was a guest and allowed access into homes.' In 1961, during the birth centenary of the Poet, *Paschatya Bhraman* was however published again containing Rabindranath's unedited letters. In the Preface to the first edition Tagore wrote that he was really not concerned whether anyone was benefitted by reading his book or not: 'I have only expressed what I felt on first seeing a foreign society. However, whether this is of any use or not, one does get to know a history of how opinions are formed and revised during the visit of a Bengali in England.'

Tagore's second trip to England lasted from August 22 to November 3, 1890. From the first published edition of *Yurop Jatrir Diary* (1893) we get an intimate portrait of Tagore as a person, especially from the 'Introduction'. His views of the orient versus the occident, of society and civilization are very significant here.

Tagore's third trip to England began in May 12, 1912 and lasted for a year and a little over four months. Here he was accompanied by his son Rathindranath and daughter-in-law, Pratima Devi. He was no longer a stranger but a familiar traveller, travelling in the same route again. So in the ship he now composed songs, reworked with the English translations and wrote letters and articles for *Tattwabodhini Patrika*. Tagore also visited several schools in England to see their methods of education. Whatever he read and saw were sent as articles/letters home. Those are now collected in *Pather Sanchoy* and *Siksha*. After staying in England for four months the Poet went to America on November 28, 1912. He stayed in different places including New York, Illinois, Urbana, Chicago, Boston and Cambridge. As a direct impact of this Europe and America trip he developed more modern ideas. On September 4, 1913 the poet boarded the ship *City of Lahore* from Liverpool and reached Bombay on October 4.

In his fourth trip to Europe Tagore arrived in England on June 5, 1920. After staying in England for four months he went to other countries of Europe. In the aftermath of World War I and his rejection of knighthood (1919), there was a marked difference in his reception now. On October 28, 1920 he reached New York along with his Irish friend, William W. Pearson. The response in America was lukewarm too and no one was ready to accept his idea of internationalism or the motto of Visva-Bharati. Returning to England on March 24, 1921, Tagore breathed a sigh of relief. By the time he returned to India in July 1921, the country was deeply involved in the non-cooperation movement.

II

As mentioned earlier, during Rabindranath's third visit to England and USA during 1912-13, he wrote some essays for publication in various Bengali journals like *Tattwabodhini Patrika, Prabasi* and *Bharati.* Rabindranath was anxious to have these collected in a travel book. In January 1915, he wrote to Ajit Kumar Chakravarty, one of the English teachers in the Ashram Vidyalaya, 'I shall feel assured if you edit *Santiniketan* and *Letters from England.*' Unfortunately nothing came of this wish till as late as 1939 when Rabindranath himself set about to prepare this book. He selected fourteen of these essays for publication. These also included some from the 1920 trip to England and USA. What is significant here is that the seventy-eight-year-old poet rewrote the essays using the colloquial *chalit* bhasha instead of the formal *sadhu* bhasha; he also revised the texts substantially. To these fourteen essays, he added an appendix which included seven letters he had written to some of the Vidyalaya teachers while he was on this trip. It is clear from this selection that Rabindranath wanted a travelogue which would compile his writings during the 1912-13 tour and his 1920 trip. In 1936, when *Paschatya Bhraman* was being prepared, his literary secretary Amiya Chandra Chakravarty had advised Rabindranath to incorporate the writings of 1912-13 and the 1920s' trips into this book. Rabindranath preferred preparing a separate book. From manuscript sources we find the title of this book was to be *Paschatya Bhraman* Volume II, but later the name *Pather Sanchoy* was chosen.

Some years after the death of the Poet, in 1946, the Visva-Bharati Publication Department decided to discard Rabindranath's own selection. They went back to the earlier formal *sadhu* bhasha version and then added all the writings of the 1912-13 tour, irrespective of whether they were related to his travel (in fact, the essays that were later included are on education and there are also some spiritual discourses) and deleted the travel writings of 1920. The seven letters included in the appendix were also abandoned. The book ceased to be a travel book. The Visva-Bharati *Rabindra Rachanabali* also followed the new edition. The Visva-Bharati Publications Department did not feel the necessity to keep record of Rabindranath's selection.

As far as the publication by the Government of West Bengal is concerned, we have two editions. The *Rabindra Rachanabali* Birth Centenary edition (Volume 10) published in Calcutta by the Government of West Bengal in 1961 has *Pather Sanchoy* based on the selections made by Tagore in 1939. Later, the 1990 edition (Volume 12) of the same *Rabindra Rachanabali*, once again published by the Government of West Bengal, contains Tagore's own selection and the revised essays in colloquial language. This includes thirteen essays, one entry titled 'Bichitra'/'Bilat-Jatrir Patra' (Letter from a Traveller to Vilayet), seven letters and nine essays as addition or supplement.

This book aims at examining both the collection of essays and related letters and bringing all of them together under one cover so that a new and comprehensive volume of *Pather Sanchoy* can be read, not only the way Tagore wanted it to be, but also as a part of a new travel text that will give the reader a more in-depth view of the poet's perception of different facets of the West. Beginning with the first article called 'Jatrar Purbapatra' (Prelude to the Journey), many of these pieces are not travel articles per se; they speak of the different philosophical issues that cross his mind, different people he meets, or the different experiences he encounters. Translated from Bengali for the first time, some of these pieces will give the reader a taste of Tagore's versatility as well.

Chapter 1

Prelude to the Journey

Our ashrama school is situated in the midst of a meadow, a place where both the old and the young, students and teachers all reside in the same room. We also have other playmates; we do not have a concealed relationship with the blue sky, the light and the breeze. Here the early morning rays of the sun fall directly upon our eyelids, the evening stars in the sky directly stare at our faces. When the storm comes, its dusty stole warns us from a very long distance. The arrival of a new season is first heralded through the new leaves on our trees. It is as if Nature does not have to wait for a moment outside our doors.

Our desire is to share this kind of a relationship with the people of the world as well. The desire of our heart is to see clearly all the seasons that come and go in the history of mankind, the rising and setting of the sun or the tumult that storm and rain create. This is possible for us because we stay far away from human habitation. Here all the information of the world is not received in a particular cookie-cutter mould; if we want we can receive them in an unadulterated form.

In order to make the relationship of our institution to the rest of the human world an open one, I feel it necessary to explore the world. We have received the invitation of that larger world. As it is not possible for all the 200 students of this school to accompany me in this grand tour, so I have decided that I shall alone attend the invitation on your behalf. Through me I shall complete all of yours travel. When I will again return to your ashrama I will be able to capture a lot of the external world in my life and bring it for you.

Once I come back I will share my experiences at leisure, but now, before departing, I want to clearly explain some of my thoughts to you.

Many people ask me why are you going for an Europe travel? I cannot find an answer to this question. If I give a simple answer that I am going because I simply want to travel, then people will think that I am dismissing the fact lightheartedly. Man is not at peace until a result is declared and an assessment made of the profit and loss involved.

Why should man venture out of home without any need is a question that can be raised in our country only. We are oblivious of the fact that the wish to venture outside is a natural instinct in man. Home has bound us up in such a manner that we are tied by many superstitions and tears once we decide to set our feet across the threshold. Thus the outside is totally beyond us while its connection with home has been completely severed. Our friends and relatives enmesh us so closely that outsiders are outsiders in the true sense of the word. That is why we have to answer so many questions even when we have to go out for a brief while. We have remained constricted for so long that we have forgotten to fly; that flying is also a pleasure is unbelievable in our country.

When I went abroad at a young age then there was an economic reason behind it. Entering the civil service or trying to be a barrister were good excuses, but that logic does not work at the age of 52. Now I will have to give some spiritual reason as an excuse.

There is need to travel for spiritual reasons—this is something which the people of our country believe in. So some people are imagining that I am travelling for that reason. That is why they are more surprised how this intention can be fulfilled in Europe. The only way to gain salvation is to travel around the pilgrimage sites in India and get acquainted with sages and other pilgrims.

I am mentioning right at the beginning that my only intention is to go out. Fortunately I have come into this world, so I should get acquainted with it as much as possible before I leave—this should be enough for me. I have got two eyes and if I can see the great world in as many different ways as possible with those two eyes, they will be satiated.

But even then I will have to admit that I too am greedy for profits; apart from happiness there is a deep desire hidden in this journey and that is to fulfil many requirements.

I believe that if any European comes with due respect to tour India then he will gain the result of a pilgrimage. I have met such Europeans and I respect them.

The reason for admiring them is not that the greatness of India reflected in their respect for our country, shines more brightly to us. I feel humble while admiring the strength of their hearts. I do not always see the ability to overcome the barrier of the unknown, acknowledge truth and accept that which is for the welfare. If we do not go into another's country then we do not get the strength to move about freely in the sphere of truth. It is a matter of weakness to accept everything that we know as the greater truth and dismiss things that we are unused to as petty or false.

When we open the door of a temple we are not used to and are able to worship truth it is then that we especially realize our devotion to truth. That worship of ours is independent; our devotion is not blindly guided by rituals.

If we visit Europe with the respect in our heart that we will witness the truth there with a free mind, then where will the Indian find a similar place for pilgrimage in the world? The respectful European pilgrims whom I have seen in India, it is not that they have not noticed our misfortune but that dirt could not blind them; they have seen the ultimate truth of India even behind her shabby exterior.

Not that there is no covering of truth in Europe. There it is covered with a bright and sunny veil unlike India. That is why it is probably more difficult to explore the innermost truth there. Guarded by brave soldiers, bejewelled ostentatiously, we may return completely amazed by the veil feeling it to be the most valuable thing there and fail to pay our homage to God who is concealed by this ostentatious cover. That only the selfsame cover is there and not Him, if I go there with this irreverence and distrust, then the huge expenses of this grand tour will be a waste.

There is a misconception about European culture that it is materialistic, completely devoid of any spirituality and people tend to believe in this kind of hearsay. Once this kind of a hearsay begins to spread it is no longer required to be true. Whatever five people say is repeated by the sixth person also and all these different voices then take the place of reason and logic.

It has to be remembered right at the beginning, whenever we see the welfare of man in any society, there is spiritual power behind it. This means man cannot get to truth through any mechanical means, it has to be acquired through spiritual means. If we see any development of man in Europe then we have to know for sure that man's spirit is behind it. It is never created out of an inanimate object; outward progress is an indication of the strength of the spirit only.

If we say that men in Europe are not expressing their spirits, they are only piling up inanimate objects—then saying this is the same as stating that large trees only shed their dry leaves and cover the ground, they do not express their lives. In reality it is the extreme life force in the large trees that helps them in shedding their leaves, the incessant rejection of dead leaves do not pronounce death. One can die only at every living moment but when death stops, that is the actual Death.

We see that in Europe man is regularly experimenting with new things and walking on the path of change—what he is accepting today, he is rejecting it the next day. He never sits quietly at one place. Many people say that this proves their lack of spirituality.

We too see constant change and death in the entire world. But have not the sages said about this world that all this emanates from joy and happiness? Isn't the divine elixir of life spreading itself unceasingly from the source of death?

If we see the external world as the ultimate then we do not get to see the inside and it also becomes impossible to know the external world truly. Europe too has an inside and a spirit which is not weak.

When I shall see the spirituality of Europe only then I shall see its truth. Then I shall know something that is not just materialistic, something that is not just learning, but the happiness.

Recently something has taken place that easily explains what I am trying to say here. A ship with 2,000 passengers on board was crossing the Atlantic Ocean. When that ship hit against a moving iceberg at midnight and was about to sink then most European and American passengers did not show keen interest in saving their own lives first and instead tried to save the lives of the women and children. This huge tragedy removed the external covering of Europe and within one moment we saw the true image of the deepest human spirit within her.

As soon as we saw this we were no longer ashamed to bow down our heads. In recognition of the human spirit, the joy of the spirit was expressed very liberally.

Within a short while of this incident a few of my friends were returning from Dhaka in a steamer. A boat sunk in the middle of the River Padma after the steamer hit it and all the three passengers fell into the river. Another boat was crossing the path nearby. All the people of the steamer shouted in unison and called the boatman to rescue those people but he didn't listen at all and just went by. There was no possibility of danger and he was nearby, so the rescue could not in any way be said to have been impossible.

I also remember another day. There had been a terrible storm at night. In the morning the velocity of the wind had reduced, but the river was still at spate. My boat was anchored on the shore of the Gorai River. Suddenly I saw the body of a woman floating past. Her hair was spread out in the water and nothing else could be seen. I called all the people on the shore and told them to take my small lifeboat and go and rescue the woman; maybe she was still alive. But no one came forward. I then said, 'I will give a reward of five rupees to each person who goes.' Only then a few people took a boat and brought her to the shore. Gradually the unconscious woman gained back her sense. Nobody would have gone if there had not been the promise of a reward.

On another day I was crossing a big lake by boat. The point where the water of the lake meets the river is used by the fishermen for helping them with their catch. They fix huge logs in the water to narrow down the outflow and because of that the force of the water increases manifold. I have seen many loaded boats face a lot of danger in such places. While trying to cross the narrow stream my boat tried to escape a collision with one of the poles and got stuck up in a very dangerous position. A few yards away the fishermen were busy fishing. We called them to come and help us but they did not bother to even glance back. Then the boatman declared a prize. With the hope that we would raise the amount the fishermen pretended not to hear. When the prize amount was raised to quite a considerable sum of money then the hindrance of the fishermen's deafness completely disappeared. But it was the result of their action that we were facing all that trouble. It need not be mentioned to the readers of our country that if this was a judge's boat then a more favourable result would have been found of this test of their hearing ability!

When a shop at Bolpur market caught fire, you surely remember that four foreign people from Kabul had helped in extinguishing that fire then and the call to the local inhabitants fell to deaf ears. You remember how they even refused to hand over the water pots because they thought that the pots would be desecrated at the hands of the outsiders.

The dearth of self-sacrifice that we see all around us is so evident that we do not need to prove it through further examples and instances. This is because whatever we might state verbally, we actually all admit to this poverty of our characters.

Isn't there any relationship between self-sacrifice and spirituality? Isn't it a symptom of the power of religion? Does spirituality mean discarding human association to remain pure in exclusion and chant names? Doesn't spiritual power grant chivalry to men?

The incident of the sinking of the *Titanic* ship has shown us many people in a bright light in the face of death. It is not that the situation has expressed the excellence of any one particular person. What is most surprising is that the millionaires who have been nurtured in the lap of Goddess Lakshmi, those who have forever considered themselves superior to others because of their wealth, those who have never faced any impediments in their pursuit of pleasure and those who have always gained advantage over others more easily during illness or in trouble, they deliberately welcomed death by letting the weak and the invalid have the first opportunity to escape. There were not just a few such millionaires in the ship.

Usually in a civilized society when trouble appears all of a sudden, man's natural base instincts reveal themselves but he can exercise self-control if he gets time to think. In the *Titanic* ship in the middle of the dark night, many of them suddenly woke up from their sleep and some casually moved outside their world of merriment to find the shadow of dark unnatural death in front of them. If at such time man is not impelled by madness and is not pushing away the weak and imbecile in trying to save himself, then it has to be understood that this bravery is not incidental or personal.

Actually the long practice of meditation of the entire race along with tremendous spiritual strength won over in this test and conquered death.

The strength that we saw collectively and so closely in this shipwreck, haven't we seen the same power in different ways and different forms in Europe? Don't we see thousands of instances of sacrificial death every day for the welfare of the nation and fellow beings? Didn't that collective sacrifice help the European civilization to raise its head like a coral island?

No society can develop if its foundation is not established upon sorrow. Those who are materialists cannot accept this sorrow; they are the slaves of inanimate objects. Those who find great pleasure in materialism, why will they discard it? Why will they accept the welfare of others above their own lives? The munificence which is proclaimed by the scriptures and which man considers to be his wealth beyond death also includes sorrow. But the munificence which is not proclaimed to be the ingredient of the scriptures, something that is not the pain of going to a pilgrimage, that which is not the boon of an auspicious communion of stars, something that is born out of the trigger of an independent spirit—can a worshipper of materialistic values ever accept that?

In Europe we have seen man accepting that sorrow and even dying, for his country, for other people, for knowledge, for love, with his independent will force.

Everything is not pure within it. A lot of it is simply show-off. But we should not demean the truth by making such allegations. In some nights we see a glorious ring around the moon. We know it is not the moon; it is a shadow, a false phenomenon. But if the moon is not in the centre then that false impression of the halo also cannot be there. In every society there is a circle around whatever is the best, borrowing the light from it, a halo of falsehood is always created. But that fake thing is not really a protest, it supports it instead. If we see fake ascetics in our country and start disbelieving all ascetics then we are befooled.

We have only read in books about extraordinary men in Europe; we haven't seen them from close quarters. The one or two people whom I have seen have not got such a place in the celebrity list in Europe. I have seen a person from Sweden for a long time and his name is Hammergrain. In that far-off country he somehow came across the name of Ram Mohan Roy in some book. He developed such a sense of devotion in him that in spite of his poverty he left his country and after a lot of difficulty crossed several oceans to land in Bengal. He did not know the language here, did not know any particular person, but he took shelter in the house of a Bengali and embraced the country of Ram Mohan Roy. The few days he survived, he underwent terrible suffering with so much devotion and endurance. Those who saw him will never forget how he dedicated his own life for the welfare of the country and how he maintained his humility. His dead body was burnt at Nimtolla Ghat and some weekly magazine had expressed distaste at the way a Hindu burning ghat was desecrated.

Everyone knows how Sister Nivedita committed self-sacrifice by dedicating her whole life for India through her devotion for Swami Vivekananda.

In both these instances we have seen that these two devotees have sacrificed their lives in such a place and under such condition where they did not have their earlier easier path in front of them; where their age-old beliefs have come across hurdles at every step on the way; where they have not only committed self-sacrifice but at every step they had to dig themselves up because their entrance was blocked on all four sides.

This power to admire the truth and to be able to cross the difficult hurdles on the way, day after day and the strength to dedicate oneself—all these characteristics they had inherited from their national practice. Can this strange power be gained from materialistic pursuits? Isn't it sufficiently spiritual enough? And I also ask, can this strength be sufficiently seen in our country?

But does that mean that there is no spirituality in our country? I do not mean that. Here also one side of spirituality has been expressed. In our country those devotees who have endeavoured to reach God either through knowledge or through devotion can easily accept the Infinity within all the material fragments of the world. Here in the case of both knowledge and intuitive understanding, age-old thoughts and devotion, their impediment has been lessened to a great extent. This is why spiritual people in our country can easily realize the link between their hearts and the Infinity.

If any foreign national comes with respect and insight to witness this strength of human nature in our country then surely he will feel satisfied and probably he can go back by fulfilling one lacunae in his own nature.

I mean to say that even we have a drawback that needs to be fulfilled and that drawback has been pulling us for a long time to the weariness of weakness.

Whenever the nationalists of our country hear this they will say, yes there is a drawback no doubt, but it is not spiritual, it is materialistic. Europe has been able to surpass all other countries of the world through this power.

I have already mentioned earlier that this can in no way be possible. No nation can develop just by accumulating materialistic wealth and no race can gain strength only with business acumen. You can pour a lot of oil in the lamp but it will not burn and even if you are an expert in making the wick, the lamp will not burn—at any cost you will have to light the fire.

Today the world is ruled by Europe through its materialistic power. This is the statement of the disbeliever. The main strength for her rule is undoubtedly religious power; it cannot be anything else.

Everyone will have to admit that the Buddhist religion is not based on materialism. But during the rise of Buddhism in India and in the following eras the way it influenced industry, science, business and imperialism had never happened before. The reason for this is that when the cloistered spirit of man is freed then it moves with happiness to flourish in all spheres with full force. Spiritualism is the central strength of man. Its nature is fulfilment. It does not want to hurt man either from inside or outside and belittle him.

I don't have the least bit of doubt that whatever the external strength of Europe might be, its basic internal strength is religion.

This religion is extremely conscious. It cannot lay aside any kind of sorrow or want in a negligent way. It is constantly attempting to curb all sorts of sorrow and trouble of man. There is a free independent mind at the centre of this attempt. The intelligence that is prompting man to drop his selfish aims, dragging him out from comfort and calling him not to fear death—who is providing such strength to him? Where is that eternal nectar stored that provides the revitalization for such liberal well wishes?

The religious seed from Jesus's life that fell over the heart of Europe has become fruitful in this way. What is the life strength within that seed? It is to accept sorrow as the ultimate wealth.

Over many centuries Europe has been listening in various chants, events and music to the idea that it is heaven's blessings that man loves and accepts all sorrows as his own. Through repeated listening this idea has become ingrained within his spirit and also beyond the conscious to his unconscious self. All the seeds of man sprout up from that secret quietness, there in that unconscious depth lies the foundation of all the wealth of man.

This is why I always see a strange thing in Europe. Those who verbally disregard Christianity and voice the success of materialism behave otherwise when time comes. They commit self-sacrifice in such a way, bear criticism and sorrow so bravely that it can be understood that even without their own knowledge they are accepting the eternal over death, and welfare above happiness.

All those people in the *Titanic* who had sacrificed their own lives and tried to save the lives of others are not all very dedicated and practising Christians; in fact there may have been some atheists or agnostics among them; but just by adopting a different religious thought could they totally dissociate themselves from the religious beliefs and practices of their race remains a question. Those who worship actually do so for their entire race. That is why even if the maximum number of indiscreet people of that race throw dust on those ascetics, even then they are not totally denied the fruit of their worship.

In our country we do not see men carrying all kinds of sorrow on their shoulders out of the love of god. However unpleasant this might sound, nevertheless we have to admit it. We have a lot of emotions emanating out of love, but the sacrifice and sorrow that also comes out of love, the desire to serve others which is only possible with bravery, that is very little visible in us. What we call the worship of god is not serving god among human beings struck with sorry and misery. We have only accepted the manifestations of love but have not accepted the sorrow that emanates out of love.

There is no spirituality in accepting sorrow as a profitable enterprise; the actual spirituality is to accept it through love.

The sorrow that a miser undergoes in hoarding his wealth, the sorrow that the man undergoes who longs for eternal salvation after death, the sorrow that a person undergoes for gaining eternal freedom and the sorrow that a sensualist undergoes sorrow to consume all worldly pleasures—none of them in any way gain complete fulfilment of desires. That acceptance only expresses the poverty of the soul. The sorrow that emanates out of love is truly the wealth of sacrifice; man overcomes death with it and elevates the strength and joy of the spirit above everything else.

It is through this divine play of sorrow that we can leave ourselves and accept the world truly. The cost of truth is this sorrow. This wealth of sorrow is the prime wealth of the human spirit. It is through this wealth that its strength is expressed and it is through this that he gains himself and others. That is why the scriptures say '*Nayamatma Balahinena Labhaha*', those who do not have the strength to accept sorrow cannot realize themselves truly.

One proof of this is that we have not been able to acquire our own country for ourselves. The people of our country do not belong to each other; the person whom the country wants does not respond to her call. The population here is not too less but that strength of number instead of expressing power actually expresses the weakness of the country.

The main reason for this is that we have not been able to embrace one another through sorrow. We have not given any value to the people of our country. If we haven't paid the price then how will we get it? Even a mother gains the child in her womb through the price of continuous service that cannot be given without sorrow. Whosoever we can accept as true and respect accordingly, we naturally pay him the price for it and no one has to coax us to do it. We have not been able to accept people all round us with the truth of our heart, and that is why we could not give up our own selves with joy either.

To see man as truth, this is the true vision of the soul and can only happen out of love. When philosophy tells us that everything is one, it is just a word; and we cannot make all things our own with mere words. The power of love that the spirit has, whose patience is infinite, self-sacrifice is whose natural pleasure; that love to serve others is naturally the only way in which we can make others our own. It is through this power that the patriot feels the Infinite spirit in the entire country, the humanist attains the same spirit within man.

The religion of Europe has initiated the nation to the love lighted by the fire of sorrow and service to others. It is through its strength that man has been easily united with other men. It is through its strength that the spark born of the fire of sorrow cannot be extinguished there and in every sphere of life hundreds of devoted men are sacrificing themselves and keeping the fire ignited in the entire country. The nectar that is being produced from that sacrificial fire is actually aiding the spread of art, science, literature, business and politics. It cannot be produced in a factory in an iron machine. It is created through persistence and meditation and that fire born of this austere devotion is man's spiritual strength, his religious strength.

That is why we can see that the way society had flourished in India during the Buddhist era, when love had embraced the idea of sacrifice, is similar to what we are witnessing of late in Europe. Medicines were arranged for the sick and even hospitals for animals had been established here, and various ways and means through which suffering of all creatures could be eliminated was also seen then. During that time the monks dismissed their own comfort and lives and travelled through difficult terrain and voluntarily embraced sorrow in order to bring peace among the foreigners and barbarians. In India, love developed on its sorrowful form during that time and gave her disciples the inspiration to be strong and great human beings. That is the reason why during that period India not only captured her own soul through religion, she could conquer the world and with her spiritual zeal could bring together materialistic as well as philosophical developments. During that period Christian civilization in Europe was even beyond dreams. The vow of sorrowful and self-sacrificial love that India possessed during that time has now become covered with artificiality and emotions but has the flame been totally extinguished? If it sees the same thing anywhere outside then will it not once again remember itself? Will not something that resides in other people's houses today be now recognized as our own thing? We have to remember that where the strength of fire is too strong, there embers will also be of a great quantity. Timidity does not have sufficient warmth; it is too little responsible and even its troublesome figure is also quite peaceful. It has to be admitted that the anger and anxiety of dissatisfaction and too much of sin that is visible in European society now is not found in our country.

But they have not accepted it casually. It hasn't overpowered their spirit; on the other hand, has always kept it alive. Beginning from the mosquitoes which carry the germ of malaria, they are constantly fighting against all the sins prevalent in their society. No one sits idle and blames it on fate; those brave men are constantly fighting even at the expense of their own lives. Recently I was reading a strange book called *London Police Courts*. In that book the underbelly of the capital city of London with its darkness, poverty and crime is described in great details. However tragic the picture might be, it also revealed over and above ideas of Christian tolerance, patience and pitiable love. There is a paean of hope in the *Gita*—even a little bit of religion and greatness rescues us from great fear. As long as religion is seen to be agile in any society, it should be considered greater than the huge quantity of misery prevalent there.

It is not that in Europe the travesty of justice in the conduct towards weaker races is not seen, but that is not overwhelming. Shame and criticism also raise their voice from the ruthless energetic greed in it. There are many courageous people there who want to protest against the injustice of the powerful and want to rectify it. Also there is no dearth of honest individuals who do not hesitate to take the sides of other distant races and suffer for them. That Indians get extensive opportunity to rule their own country—a few such Indians are present in our country who are occupied with that intent—but from whom have they got the training and who is their real aide? Those who accepting criticism from relatives, acknowledging all adversity are trying to restrict the selfishness of their fellow people in the name of religion, which country do these people belong to? They seem to be very few in number but seen through the eyes of truth they are not so few. This is because they do not end in themselves. They are part of a visible and invisible tradition in the country. Not that they do the same work or are together at the same time, but they are the ones who are the essential source of justice in society. They are the Kshatriyas, they have worn the shield to relieve and protect all the weak people of the world. Those who have suffered sorrow in order to save people from the world of sorrow, those who have accepted death in order to take man to paradise, they are following the footsteps of their deceased spiritual leaders who have treaded the humiliating, bloody and difficult terrain. They bring in the nectar of the transcendental river Mandakini to the heart of the entire race.

We always comfort ourselves by saying that we are a religious and spiritual race. We do not pay any attention to external things; that is exactly why we are weak in the outside world. We want to reduce our shame about this external weakness. Many of us verbally boast that poverty is our asset.

Poverty is actually the asset of those who have the power to grab wealth. The asset that has no value is not an asset at all. This is why the poverty born of sacrifice is an ornament not that which is born of need. Poverty is an asset of Lord Shiva, but the poverty of one who is inauspicious by nature [Alakshmi] is very ugly. Those who are always unhappy because they don't get sufficient food to eat; those who want to somehow save their lives but do not have the strength to adopt the difficult means through which it is possible and hence fall down on the ground repeatedly; those who fleece the poor whenever they get an opportunity because they themselves are poor; and those who are themselves disabled but hurt others whenever they get a chance and power to do—for none of them is poverty an asset.

All our sorrow, poverty and humiliation we have never regarded as reward for our religious mindedness and therefore have not been able to extend our sphere of spirituality. We have encapsulated it within our personal religious practices, we have not collected all human beings together at its call. Wherever the blind torture of social rule has crushed in the stony grinder man's ability for judgment and independent thinking, making everything alike—it is there that constricted religious ideas and an unconsciousness has turned us into inanimate objects suitable for slavery. We believe even now that our troubles will end with legal aid and we will become true human beings when we get a seat to rule the nation. But national deliverance is not a mere mechanical tool. As long as man is not prepared to pay the price from within himself, till then '*Nanyaha Pantha Vidyate Ayanaha*', no other path is known for eternal life.

That is why I was saying that if we go to Europe with the aim of a pilgrimage then our journey will not be in vain. There also we have our gurus, and that guru is the enlightened inner strength of human society. We have to seek that spiritual leader everywhere with due respect; he cannot be just visible as soon as we open our eyes. It is also possible that we do not get to meet the spiritual leader of that society and we come back with our blindness and pride by not seeing him. It is also not surprising that we come back with a strange idea that England's power is being created by her parliament, that Europe's wealth is being produced in factories and all the glory of the western countries are reliant on weapons of war, merchant ships and external material wealth. Those who do not feel the real inner strength within themselves will easily tend to believe that the power is an external manifestation and all our needs will also be fulfilled if we get the opportunity to seize those things. But, '*Jenaham Namrita Syam Kimaham Tena Kurjam*' that is not the case *(as you sow so you reap)*. These are the inner words of Europe. Europe also knows that she is not great due to her railways, telegraphs and factories. That is why it has accepted the truth like a brave warrior. The more mistakes it makes, the more failures it meets, the more Europe is beginning everything with renewed and double vigour, never letting things go at any cost. Sometimes misfortune appears, flames arise due to conflict, even gall is sometimes churned out of the ocean along with the nectar, but they are never accepting what is bad. They have their weapons ready, their soldiers are fearless and with the training in truth they have developed the strength even to overcome death. We have been lazy to face the truth; we are not interested in pursuing it; and we have immersed ourselves entirely within the confine of the regular ties of building of home and hearth imagining them to be the sanctuary of truth. That is why when difficult days arrive, when we have no other option but to pursue the path of truth, then we cannot rouse ourselves in any way and cannot sacrifice ourselves. Even then we assume play to be important as work; we imitate things and expect to reap real benefits. We cannot keep alive the flame of false inspiration, cannot finish the duties prescribed to us and instead entwine ourselves in a lot of philosophical thoughts and repeatedly fail in our mission. That is why if we accept the responsibility of truth entirely like a brave warrior, have a sincere dedication towards that truth, gain the most valuable assets of life at the expense of all sorrow and hardship, work towards the welfare of man with intelligence, heart and diligence and take up the difficult vow of worshipping God through service to man, the trip to Europe cannot be fruitless for the pilgrim. Of course for that one needs to have a sort of respect in the mind and consider a holistic development of man as an indication of true spiritual success.

I know there has been a clash between our welfare and that of Europe and because of that we are suffering deep anguish and pain both internally and externally. That pain is actually the face of our spiritual poverty and even if it forms a repentance for our accumulated sins, it still remains painful. For us, those who form the pretext for this pain, we get a taste of their meanness and cruelty in various ways. We are also seeing everyday how they have concealed their meanness through great hypocrisy and have refused to accept the greatness of other nations through blindness and ego. That is the reason why we feel hesitant to accept the truth of Europe with our bruised heart. We do not trust their religion and we criticize their civilization to be too materialistic. Not only that, we are scared that we may worship the might of the mighty as something true and make ourselves impure before it by falling on the ground, unable to accept the glory of others along with our own glory; or we may in the slothness of self-confidence discard our own truth and in the emptiness of imitation become a shadow of another's body and an echo of another's voice and make ourselves worthless in this world; or we may hold to a strange hallucination of thought that disclaiming oneself to give credibility to another is the true means of liberation.

All these obstacles are there and that is why the path to seek the truth is actually a pilgrimage. We will have to overcome all falsehood and move forward, tolerate all obstacles on the way and yet keep on progressing; leave behind all the false burden of personal ego and keep moving but treasure the allowance of self-respect that we gain on our path. Actually it is through all these obstacles that I can expect my pilgrimage to be completely successful. That is because we do not consciously accept things that we get easily. But the success of gaining anything completely lies in a more complete realization of one's conscience. In other words all that we get to acquire truly helps us to realize ourselves as true. If we do not do that and acquire only externally then it is illusion, it is false.

[First published in *Tattwabodhini Patrika*, *Asharh* issue, 1319 B.S.]

Chapter 2

The City of Bombay

Yesterday afternoon I went out to get a glimpse of the city of Bombay. My first impression was that the city of Bombay has a distinctive feature; Calcutta has no such special feature, as if it has somehow been haphazardly patched together.

The fact is that the sea has given a particular shape to the city of Bombay. The city clings to the sea through its semicircular beaches. The pull of the sea seems to be at work in all the streets and lanes of Bombay. I feel that the sea functions like a gigantic heart; it is pulling life force into the veins and arteries of the city and sustaining it. The sea has made this city look out to the vast beyond forever.

The River Ganges was once one of Calcutta's ties with nature. Its flow was the open path that carried news from distant lands towards unknown mysteries. It was the one window of the city from where you could look out and realize that the world was not confined to this settlement. But the once natural strength of the Ganges has been dissipated—it has been dressed up in such tight clothes on both its banks and its waist band has been tightened so that the Ganges seems to be the image of a liveried footman of the city. One cannot figure out now how once upon a time it could have had functions apart from transporting huge bales of jute on barges. Haven't the feelers of dolphins hid themselves in shame in the spiky jungle of masts of ships?

The special glory of the sea is that it serves man but does so without wearing the yoke of slavery on its neck. The business of shipping jute cannot hide from view the blue jewel in its mighty heart. That is why the image of an ocean flowing next to this city is something that is indefatigable. On the one hand, it spreads the fruit of man's work around the world; on the other, it keeps out of sight man's feeling of exhaustion, dispersing the sense of leisure before the possibility of endless work.

So when I saw hundreds of decked up men and women sitting on the beach, I liked the sight very much. They could not ignore the call of the ocean that relaxing afternoon. They do their work close to the lap of the sea and also enjoy themselves in her lap. In our Calcutta we have the Eden Gardens, but she is the daughter of a miser—there is no lure in her voice. In that garden created by the men of the Raj, there is much disciplining and many things are forbidden. But the ocean was not created by someone and so there is no way that one can fence it in. This is why there are regular festivities and such merriment taking place on the beaches of Bombay regularly. Calcutta has no such place for this kind of an uninhibited enjoyment.

What delighted me most of all was the sight of the men and women who had assembled there all around. The poverty of the Calcutta scene, bereft as it is of womenfolk strikes one here. We see only half of mankind there, and that is why we do not see it in its joyous elements. Not being able to delight in the sight is surely a sort of punishment.

Surely, the lack of such sights constrains the minds of people and has prevented them from blossoming. How unfortunate are those human beings who cannot savour the very natural beauty of the view of men, women and children all gathered on the beach in an afternoon to partake of the same happiness. That sadness which is habitual keeps us in a state of stupor but there is no doubt that the losses we suffer in the process keep piling up everyday. Men and women meet all the time within the four walls of a room, but can only such meetings suffice? There is a wide open world out there that exists for men to meet one another—cannot we enjoy the simple delight of meeting in such a natural ambience?

Our car came and parked in front of a garden in the hills of Matheran. The small garden was encircled with benches on all sides. Here also I saw housewives sitting with their relatives and enjoying the natural breeze. Apart from some Parsi ladies, there were also Marathi women with vermilion on their foreheads, a sort of loveliness writ large on their faces. That one's existence is an imperilled one, that one has to protect oneself from the gaze of anyone around—this idea is least in their minds. I kept thinking to myself how the burden of constraint had come off the head of the whole country and how compared to us, the lifestyle here has become easy and beautiful in many ways.

If the simple right to partake the natural air and light of the earth is prevented, mankind erects an unnatural barrier for itself—this truth can be perceived by anyone observing the always hesitant and helpless state of the women of our country. The long history of cruelty against the women of our country becomes evident when we view our women in railway stations. Strolling in this garden at Matheran, I tried to remember our own Beadon Park and Goldighi—how wretched their miserliness appeared now to be.

When butterflies go to look for honey in the garden of flowers, they are not inclined to show-off; as a matter of fact, they are then too rapt in their work. But this does not mean that they don black overcoats for going to office then. When I see the assorted colours of the clothes that people wear here, this is the thought that occurs to me. I do not believe that there is a dire necessity for making our working atmosphere deliberately drab. The colours in the turbans, borders and saris of the people of Bombay expresses happiness and enlivens the happiness in their lives. No sooner had I left Bengal, I began observing this phenomenon. The farmer who is working in the field has a turban on his head and a coat frock on his body. Needless to say, the women are as colourfully apparelled. This external difference between us and the people here does not seem insignificant to me. It is this external difference from us that has led me to respect them. They do not neglect themselves; they make themselves remarkable through appearing neat. This is an obligation men owe to other men; if this penchant for dressing up is absent then man's bareness expresses itself in a very ugly manner. If each person does not try and protect his own society from the squalor associated with the failure to dress up because of habitual insensitivity, our slackness will lower the esteem of our country in the eyes of the world.

I noticed one other thing in the city of Bombay. This was the wealth of the locals. How many Parsi, Muslim and Gujarati traders' names I saw emblazoned on the walls of mansions! So many names inscribed so prominently cannot be seen anywhere in Calcutta. There the wealth stems from salaried service and the zamindari system, hence it is very drably displayed. The wealth of the zamindars is like stagnant water; it shrinks with use and gets polluted through profligacy. We do not find the expression of human strength there; there is no new flow of revenue either. It is for this reason that the people in Bengal feel so timid despite whatever wealth they possess. I see that the Marwaris, Parsis, Gujaratis and Punjabis are more liberal in their donations, but Bengalis are the least charitable of people. The donation books in our region are like local cows—they have hardly any place to graze. Our countrymen have not been able to experience wealth hence their miserliness is ugly, while their notion of extravagance is even more horrifying. It makes me happy to see that while the lifestyle of the rich people here is simple, they are liberal with their wealth.

[First published in *Tattwabodhini Patrika*,
Asharh issue, 1319 B.S.]

Chapter 3

Water and Land

We live on land but we have the ocean all around us. Man is in the middle of these two contradictory forces of water and land. But how daring is the spirit of man! The water whose banks he could not even see he did not perceive it as a deterrent and instead started sailing upon it.

The water that is friendly towards man flows from within the land. The rivers are like our sisters on the shore. They walk such long distances to the stone-embankment of the river bank carrying water upon their waists. They are the ones who quench our thirst, arrange for our meals. But what great enmity we have with the ocean! Its endless water is as thirsty as the Sahara desert. It is strange that in spite of it man could not be deterred. Like the blue buffalo of Lord Yama, the deity of death, she is constantly shaking her horns but could not make man recede backwards.

The world is divided into two parts—one that provides shelter and the other that does not. One is stationary, the other always in motion; one quiet and the other terrible. The child of the world who has dared to accept both these forms is actually the winner of all the treasures that the world possesses. Those who have bowed down to obstacles and have moved away in fear, will never attain the wealth of Lakshmi. That is why it is stated in our Puranas that Lakshmi is *chanchala*—always on the move—she has risen from the restless ocean and has not been born in our fixed earth.

Lakshmi has a vow that she will always give shelter to the brave person. That is why she has spread this huge fear of waves in front of man. She will succumb only when man can cross it. Those who sit on the shore and go to sleep listening to the sound of the waves and do not venture into the ocean or do not spread out the sails and cross over, remain deprived of the wealth of the world.

I kept on thinking about this when our ship churned the angry heart of the blue ocean into foam and sailed towards the shoreless western horizon. I could clearly see that the day the Europeans conquered the ocean, the very same day they also welcomed Lakshmi. And those who remained stuck at one place and did not proceed further, just stagnated there.

The earth binds everybody. Like an exceedingly doting mother she does not allow her children to venture far away. She feeds them bellyful of rice and vegetables and then spreads out the shady deep green end of her sari and puts them to sleep. If the child wants to go out of the house then she tries to prevent by citing lots of fear and superstition.

But man has to go far. His mind is so large that it cannot move freely when confined to only nearby places. If you keep it enclosed by force within that then a lot of it gets excluded. Those who have been able to venture far away have found success. The ocean in front of man shows him that distant path; it is constantly alluring him to venture towards the unattainable. Those who responded to that call and moved out are the ones who conquered the world. The melodic tune of Lord Krishna's flute plays within the blue waters and beckons man to leave the shore and go out.

There is the sign of fulfilment on one side of the world and incompleteness on the other. The shore has been built and the little building and rebuilding that occur within it is trivial and hence not noticeable. The architect of that little change is also water. But the task of creation in the ocean bed is still incomplete. The rivers which labour for the ocean carry tons of mud and sand from distant places and deposit it here. And millions of small shells, corals and insects keep on constantly supplying the ingredients for such masonry work. A period has been inserted towards the land; at least a semi-colon; but there is no sign of any end towards the ocean. In the uncertain and eternal restlessness that is dark and mysterious and spread as wide as the sky it is very difficult to ascertain what is actually happening, and know its direction. This ocean is turbulent, untiring and its energy is unending.

That race of people on this earth who have especially welcomed this ocean have also found the unceasing effort of the ocean in their character. They are the ones who keep on saying that the aim of man's life is not to reach an ultimate goal but it is just spreading oneself out and moving along this ceaseless movement. Diving into uncertainty without any fear they go on garnering new wealth. They cannot remain stationary at some corner, building a nest. The distant beckons them and the things that are difficult to attain attracts them. Waves of dissatisfaction keep on hammering endlessly upon these hearts and engage continuously in the processes of creation and destruction. At night when the entire world sleeps, even then in their factory-room the lamp-like eyes do not wink. They are constantly fighting with rest and do not accept any conclusion.

And those people who have built their dwelling on land are constantly saying, 'No more, there is no necessity.' Not only do they restrict their hunger, they want to kill hunger itself and throw it out. They want to create permanence from what little they have got and so have been creating the barrier of tradition and certainty all around them. They plead and say, 'Do whatever you want, but don't try to cross the ocean because if you enjoy the ocean breeze once and get a taste of the uncertain, then it will stoke up the intoxication of dissatisfaction within human heart and then it will be difficult to avert it.' In order to prevent the flute of the black ocean bringing in the melody of the new unknown through some restless wind there is a constant effort to raise the height of the artificial walls reaching inside the house.

But I believe that time has arrived to accept the complete independence of ocean and land and do away with this discrimination between them. Both these elements combine together to form the world of man. If the separation between the two is kept alive, then it is dangerous for man. Then why has this separation been continuing for all these days? That is because they wanted to attain each other through austerity like Hara and Gouri (Shiva and Parvati). On the one hand you see him sitting naked and still in a trance-like state, and on the other Gouri is decking herself up with the new flowers of spring. All the gods in heaven are waiting for their holy union otherwise no good result will be born.

We the people of the land have accepted the complete and final image of the divine as truth. There would have been no harm in that. But we want to dismiss his dissemination as false—that is undesirable. If we dismiss part of the truth as false then the rest of the truth also turns false. We accepted stability and happiness but refused to accept strength and sorrow. That is why we insulted the Queen and yet couldn't save ourselves by praising the King; for thousands of years truth has been hurting us in different ways.

The people of the ocean have accepted the expanse of the divine as ultimate truth. They are determined that in no circumstance they will accept conclusion. This is why they are accepting everything from the outside but because they are never satisfied they are not gaining anything. Similarly, in regard to theoretical knowledge they have started saying that there is no direction of truth, there is only motion. They want something to turn to but do not know what. This is like that kind of an ocean where there is neither shore nor bottom. What exists are only the waves—they neither quench your thirst, nor help to grow crops, but only rock you.

We saw happiness and called sadness as something false and elusive. But nothing can be excluded from complete truth; if the east does not meet the west then the east seems false; so does the west. '*Anandodbhava Khalvimani Bhutani Jayante*'—just as it is true that everything is being born from joy or happiness, '*Sa Tapahotapyat*', it is also true that everything is created from austerity and sorrow. Just as songs that are beyond a particular place and time provide joy to the heart of the singer so also is true the sorrow that he feels to express his song within time and place. To accept both this joy and sorrow, closure and expansion, the eternally old and new, the fertile land and the ocean full of sorrow and tears together is to realize the truth.

This is why I see that those who do not accept the culmination but only go after development grow wild and run towards accidental death; at every step their ship hits into the blind mountain of occasional revolt. And those who claim development to be false and only consider the culmination to be true are overwhelmed by impotency and weakness and lie in bed to die.

But with the passage of time one day when the vehicle on the land and the ship on the ocean will reach the same harbour and both sides will exchange their goods, then both of them will be saved. Otherwise no one can do away with poverty with the help of only one's own goods; business or trade cannot carry on without exchange and if the trade does not go on then there will be no sign of Lakshmi, the goddess of wealth.

Because this trade can unite man with one another, the wealth of the world has been scattered in different regions.

The division between male and female in animals, have exposed them to myriad pain and pleasure and the quality of their lives have developed excellence by going through these. In a similar way in human nature, some men's hold on stability and others' to movement have led us today to expect a union which will enrich civilization of man in many different ways.

Arabian Sea
Jaisthya 16, 1319 B.S.
[First published in *Prabasi, Sravana* issue, 1319 B.S.]

Chapter 4

Crossing the Ocean

Crossing the dock, I boarded the ship. I have boarded a ship several times on earlier occasions but each time I have felt a sort of hesitation in the beginning. This hesitation is not because of being among unknown people in unknown places. I feel the separation between the ship and my own life very deeply. The people who have built this ship, those who are sailing in it, they are the masters of this ship—I have just got a place here by purchasing a ticket. For generations so many sailors have left their invisible trail on the unmarked paths of this ocean; so many hundreds of deaths have repeatedly occurred to make this path easier. That I can freely eat and move about in this ship during the day and sleep peacefully at night—can this reliability be procured only through money? Behind it lie so many layers of thought, so much accumulated courage, whereas we have nothing to offer yet.

When I see these English men and women playing on the deck, sleeping and gossiping, then I can see that they are not just on the ship; they are also relying on the strength of their fellow beings. They surely know that what needed to be done has been done, and what needs to be done, will also be done; for that their entire nation stands as a security. For any life risk that might occur, they not only have the captain but the entire nation which, with its natural endeavour and untiring alertness, is prepared to fight against death till the last moment. Thus they are moving so freely and cheerfully on that firm ground without bothering to consider the waves on all sides. Here they are receiving what they have already given; and we, who have not yet given anything, are also taking it. Thus as we are crossing the ocean we are leaving debts behind us. That is why I feel hesitant to sit on the deck along with these English passengers.

On land we use a lot of foreign items but that does not cause a sense of poverty in our minds; on the ship it seems that we are taking even more. This is not just a factory—there are human beings in it. The people who are navigating the ship are doing it with their own bravery and strength; if we had the sense to realize how we are relying on their humanity, then along with the clinking of money with which we had bought our tickets would also have blended the sound of other values as well. Today I feel a sorrow in my heart because they are steering the ship with their hearts while we are travelling by just paying some money. How and when shall we be able to cross the great ocean that lies between the two of us? We have not yet begun; there are still so many human sacrifices to be made, so many ties to be broken, so many beliefs to be trampled upon. Whenever

I think of this I understand that making a few paper boats and blowing a few speeches on the toy sail will not lead us anywhere.

Severing ties with the shore we are now in the middle of the blue ocean. I feared that as a creature of the land I would not be able to tolerate the sway of the ocean but the seasonal turbulence of the Arabian Sea has not yet begun. Not that there is no disturbance at all; the westerly wind is blowing and the waves are lashing against the bow of the ship. But this has not caused any revolt within my body. So my first encounter with the ocean has begun as an address of love; it has not shaken out and emptied the poetry out of the poet; the dance of my blood can keep good pace with the tune in which she is playing the beat. If she suddenly wishes to become violent and play the tune of destruction I shall not be able to raise my head. But it seems in this trip she is not going to apply the ridicule of her tumultuous laughter over this scared disciple.

So I spend my days holding on to the railing of the ship and looking at the water. Our journey began towards the end of the bright moonlight. The night over the ocean is just like the ocean itself; I stand still and watch the grand union of two infinites; quietly listening to the conversation of stasis with movement, silence with sound spread across the sky. I like to watch the way in which the waves fall and rise on both sides of the ship. It seems as if the ship is cutting through the core of a flower and the white petals are instantly spreading out on either side.

In this quiet night I have the deep sound of the ocean in front of me, while behind me is the constant fun and frolic and laughter of the passengers of the ship. Every time I have travelled in a ship I have felt that the passengers did not have a moment to look at the serene eternity that surrounds our little lives. Their attachment to life is so strong that even for a single moment they cannot cross the distance required to understand the truth of life. This is why their ceremony of worship is such a grand affair—as if they have to detach themselves from one place for a moment to reach the other. If this ship was full of Indian travellers, then even amid the day's work and pleasure we would have seen people pressing their palms together unashamedly and paying obeisance to eternity; even amidst petty laughter and gossip, they would very easily break into religious songs. The here and the eternity, the created and the Creator are all blended together.

The idea that the union of both these elements results in complete truth is so easily ingrained in our minds that we do not feel any hesitation about it. But I cannot imagine that these English passengers would break into religions songs within the course of a small break in their merrymaking, and while gambling on the deck if they suddenly lift their eyes and see one of their fellow passengers sitting on a stool praying, then they will all be very disappointed and consider him out of his mind. This is why we do not find the benign gleam of spiritual awareness in their lives; a one-sided fierceness reveals itself in their work and conversation instead.

This ship has such wonderful arrangements. We do not know the whole mystery behind the way she constantly fights her way through time and space. Day and night I can feel the beat of its hard iron heart going up and down. Where the fire of her stomach is burning and the hot steam churning in her veins, all the power and effort that is there is hidden from our eyes. Up here amid the plentiful leisure and laziness we are made aware of the timings for food and bath through the occasional sound of a bell. I keep on thinking about the place where they prepare the meals for all these 150 to 200 passengers. That also takes place behind our eyes. We can neither hear their sound, nor smell anything. When we go and sit at the dining table then everything is decorated and ready; the food items are continuously served like the easy flow of a river.

What is really worrying is that while crossing such a huge ocean these people do not accept the least bit of inconvenience or any little shortage in food and pleasure. They are unwilling to accept any form of excuse and at all conditions want to keep their personal needs at the highest level. As a result, even their impossible requirements are met with. It is only people who do not have the courage to demand, who somehow spend their days compromising with wants and say '*Ardhang Tyajati Panditaha*', half of what they have should be given to pundits. As a result, even from that half, half portion is excluded and the pundit remains engulfed in his own learning.

But if one thinks of taking all the advantages, then one has to carry a heavy burden. Every little arrangement for comfort takes up such a lot of space! They have the power to carry such weight and there they do not feel the slightest shame about it. In this instance I am reminded of the system in our school. There also arrangements have to be made to feed 200 people four times a day. There is no dearth of effort but even then shouting continues from four in the morning to one o'clock at night. There is nothing more than bare essentials and though the arrangements are reduced as much as possible, the weight of the wastage does not decrease. The confusion increases, garbage is accumulated and no one knows what to do with the rice water, vegetable peels and the extra food. Gradually one can stop thinking about it, entrust oneself to inanimate nature and somehow spend the days. We are unable to say with emphasis that this cannot be done because if you say it you will have to bear the burden. In the end, we go to the roots and see that neither do we have the confidence nor the power to bear such burden. This is why we can bear only sorrow and inconvenience, but are unwilling to bear any responsibility.

A highly-placed railway engineer is travelling with us. He told me, 'I have tried very hard to collect locks, keys and many other small essential items from our country for the railway department. But every time I see that they cost more and are not of good quality.' The cost of merchandise and salary is increasing on the one hand but the products that are manufactured cannot compete with the market prices of the world. He further added that those factories that are run by European management have very little impact on the people of our country. Again, those under local management cannot extract full labour—most of them do not have the power to make people work with their maximum strength. This is why though the wages are low, the price of things cannot be reduced. The power that is used is not comparable to the number of people working.

Though it does not sound nice, this is the sight visible wherever you look in our country. All kinds of work have become difficult there and the only reason for it is that we do not get the complete man. Hence we have to work with more people and at the same time it is beyond our power to make them work in a regulated manner and satisfy them. This is also the reason why the paraphernalia of work becomes several times more important than the actual work; there is more waste than the arrangement and the holes in the boat go on increasing in such number that more labour is expended in spilling out the water than the actual rowing of the boat. Anyone who has attempted any sort of work in our country will vouch for it.

I asked that engineer, 'Are not prices going down in your country because of joint business and quality factories?' 'It might be so,' he replied. 'But in any country we cannot say that joint business comes first and development follows later. If men are inclined to joint business then it happens in itself.' He added, 'I have seen the rise and decline of many local joint businesses near Madras in South India. I have seen that no one has the loyalty or the sincerity required to run such an enterprise; everyone only looks after his own individual needs. For this reason, nothing can be constructive. If this stern loyalty is expedited in our national character then all kinds of collaborative efforts are possible.'

I liked his words. It is not true that prosperity comes through programmes because at the very root of it we have man. Each work in our country begins by depending on one particular man but after that people who accept that same work depend a lot on it but do not turn out to be so dependable. This is because they do not look so much at the work as they do look after themselves. For every little thing their clenched fist becomes loose; instead of crossing over the impediment they try to leave it and run away while constantly thinking that given another situation he would have got better results. This is how things get scattered—from one it results into five pieces and all the five turn out to be failures. Until the time comes when people will accept both success and failure bravely and also complete their defined job with utmost loyalty, any attempt at joint business venture or group welfare project will be impossible in our country.

This loyalty does not come from intelligence; it is generated from the heart, from life. With what strength does man carry himself in total failure? Calculating the profit and loss in one's life seems petty compared to the attraction of the entire life. If this was not true then man would have committed suicide to free himself of trivial reasons, trivial losses and trivial unhappiness. Thus, if we do not have some amount of respect for the work towards which we have dedicated our lives; if we are not attracted to it beyond all calculations; if we cannot stand for it with due respect even when we are defeated; if we do not have the strength to hold the flag of success high even at the time of death; if we do not totally neglect the lesson by which we can come out of the magic circle as Abhimanyu did; then we shall not be able to create anything, nor protect it. In spite of all gain and loss, all defeat, first of all we need the strength to say, 'This is ours, so this is mine.' After that, some day or another, we shall be able to overcome the sea of impediments in whatever programme we follow.

Nowadays even in the western countries we hear that European life is depleting itself by attempting too much of work and it is not entirely false. I have mentioned earlier that Europe is determined not to accept any deficiency or drawback. She has unlimited faith in her own strength, to express that strength in its full glory and achieve the impossible. But even then, there is a limit to power. We cannot say that we will light the candle very brightly and at the same time not let the wick burn.

This is why the more the lifestyle demands increase in the western countries, the more they burn themselves. Determined not to compromise with comfort and convenience, their burden constantly grows larger and larger in size. This burden creates a pressure somewhere. Wherever this pressure is created, an equal amount of sadness is also being generated but without equal amount of compensation. In order to maintain equilibrium in this affected society, it therefore tries to raise its head intermittently like a volcanic earthquake. The constant increase in gadgets for the comfort of man is actually replacing man himself. Where is the end to this? Man is turning himself into a machine for fulfilling all his material wants. In which leisure moment will he find himself? He has got to put a full stop at any cost and say, 'Here are my gadgets, now I must rescue myself. I will have to provide whatever is essential for me, but all these are unnecessary.'

This means whenever the efforts of man go on at the same momentum, he reaches a point where he becomes the cause of his own unsuccessfulness. The road to complete fulfilment is not smooth. This is why what pains Europe today does not pain us. Europe has constructed her physical body and is trying to establish the spirit inside it. Our spirits have lost the body and are roaming fruitlessly around the earth like ghosts. Where is the external manifestation of that spirit? There is the religion of God in it, so it cannot live without spreading its wealth. It wants to manifest itself in different ways—through the state, business, society, art, literature and religion. But where are the ingredients here? Where is the control over those ingredients? I find that if we try to bind that physical body in one place, it becomes loose on the other—if it remains dense for a moment, the next moment it evaporates. So today we must understand this body mechanism by whatever means possible; we must understand at any cost that a soul without a body is never true because the body is part of the soul. It is that part which gives us movement, power and death, but the soul gets its stability, happiness and eternity only along with the body. It is this incompleteness in creating the body that makes the ugly soul of our country wail through century after century. By distancing the external truth our internal spirit is constantly creating only dreams. It is losing its weight. This is why there is no proof or limit to its superstitions; this is why it sometimes plays with truth as if it is illusion; and sometimes takes illusion and tries to use it like truth.

Arabian Sea
Jaisthya 17, 1319 B.S.
[First published in *Tattwabodhini Patrika*,
Sravana, issue, 1319 B.S.]

Chapter 5

Journey

Once upon a time man was wild and so were horses. Man did not know how to run but the horses would run as fast as the wind. How graceful was its movement, how limitless its freedom. Man would just look at it and feel jealous. He would think, 'If I had such four legs which were as fast as lightening, then distance would not be any consideration for me. I would go and conquer distant places.' Man really envied the thrill and the joy of running that was expressed in the body of the horse.

But man was not satisfied just sitting and craving for it. Sitting under the shade of a tree he kept on thinking how he could acquire the four legs of the horse. No one else except man was capable of having such weird ideas. 'I am a two-legged animal, can I somehow get two more legs? Hence this rule can never be violated that I shall walk slowly forever one step at a time and the horse will run very fast.' But the perturbed mind of man could not anyhow accept this.

One day he caught a wild horse with a noose. He got hold of his mane and sat on his back. Thus he added the four legs of the horse to his body. It took him a long time to bring those four legs under his control—he fell down several times, died several deaths, but never surrendered under any circumstances. He was determined to seize the power of the horse as his own. In the end he won. The slow-moving man captured fast movement and started using it for his own needs.

After walking on the land, at one point of time man found that the ocean was in front of him and he could not proceed further. He could neither gauge the depth of the blue water nor could he see the shore. Also millions of waves raised their pointed fingers and threatened man saying, 'If you proceed further then I will see you. Here your dictates won't work.' So man sat on the shore and kept staring at this endless prohibition. But there was also a great call within this prohibition. The waves danced with a loud laugh and unlike the land they could not be harnessed. Looking at them it seemed as if lakhs and lakhs of children had been freed after school—shouting and jumping and even then dissatisfied, they would want to kick the earth like a football and make it fly in the sky. After watching this man could not sit peacefully on the shore. The turbulence of the ocean also instigated the rush of blood within him. So he wished to own this boundless rush of water and widespread freedom. He started eyeing this limitless joy of the ocean. Like the waves he desired to conquer the horizon.

But how could his strange wish be fulfilled? His power was restricted up to the shore and all his desires had to end at this point. But the point where it is wanted that man should end his desire he gets more excited. Under no circumstance was he willing to accept any obstruction as the terminating point.

At last one day he managed to conquer the waves as he did with the mane of the horse and started to ride upon it. The angry ocean shook its back. There was no limit to the number of men who were drowned or were dead. At last one day man managed to tame this wild ocean. It bowed down and surrendered itself from shore to shore.

Today after boarding the ship I realize what is the nature of that being called man who is associated with the huge ocean. We are just small creatures silently standing at one end of the ship, but everything, every distance has come and blended with me. By standing motionless here I have captured even the distant shores that are as yet not visible today. The impediment is itself carrying me on its back and helping me to move forward. The entire ocean is mine, as if it is my huge body, my extended wings. Whatever impediments we might have had have been turned into our path of movement. It is as if we have divine instructions that we have to seek our means of salvation from it as well. Those who have obeyed these instructions have been set free in this world. For those who disobeyed, the world has turned into a prison for them. Their own village has encircled them, the corner of the house has tied them up and at every step the chains around their feet make a jingling sound.

I am sailing in a joyous mood. I was scared that the motion of the waves would make me sick but that fear has been dispelled now. The little bit of swaying that I am now feeling seems to be caressing instead of hurting me. The ocean is carrying me on its lap just like a careful father carrying a weak child. For this reason, instead of feeling any difficulty moving around, I have been enjoying the pleasure of movement.

I have come outside simply because I want to enjoy this pleasure of travelling. This pressure to travel, to go outside had made me restless since a long time. Many a day when I sat alone on the first floor balcony of our ashram dwelling and looked in front towards the sky towering over the sal trees, then it seemed as if that sky was pointing its fingers towards the distance and sending me a signal. Though that sky was silent, yet the beckoning from all the unknown mountains, rivers and forests had filled up its blue expanse. That silent sky used to carry the message of those distant murmurs and sounds from far away and bring them to me. It would always tell me, 'Come on, come outside.' That movement was not out of some necessity but for the sheer pleasure of travelling.

The soul always wants to travel, that is its nature. It dies if it does not travel. That is why it goes on moving either for necessity or for pleasure. You have seen the ducks that flock on the shoals of the Padma. They leave their nests that are located next to some lonely lake encircled by the rugged Himalayan peaks and after flying for many days and nights they arrive on the sandy banks of the Padma. During winter, the snow and mist become terrible and the

Himalayas hurry them up to begin their journey in search of a new home. Therefore during that time the ducks have a necessity to begin their journey towards the south. But apart from that necessity there is an additional thing. This flight of crossing so many distant mountains and rivers enhances the spirit of these birds and makes them happy. The call of changing their nests frequently shakes up their entire lives and gives them an opportunity of experiencing life anew.

I too received a call from within me to change my abode. Coming out of the enclosure in which I was living at present, I too had to go somewhere else. Move on, move on, move on. Let us keep on moving like the waterfall, the waves of the ocean, the birds at dawn, the light at sunrise. That is why the world is so huge, the earth so diverse, the sky so infinite. That is why the atoms and molecules are dancing all around the universe and countless galaxies with their own camps of light are moving across the sky like wandering Bedouins without knowing their destination. There is no rule in the universe that one should build a nest and settle down permanently at one place. That is why the call of death is nothing but just a call to change the dwelling place. It won't allow life to remain enclosed within any traditional wall in any way. Death comes because it will let life lead its own path to survival.

That is why I am travelling now. Like the fairy-tale prince who just set out one day to cross the seven seas, I too have ventured into the outside world today. The princess is fast asleep and she cannot be woken up from her slumber. We need the golden wand. Sitting at one place and living within the same rules and habits life begins to stagnate. Man becomes unconscious; clinging to his own bed he cannot realize the vast world. So we need to find out the golden wand and venture out into the distant lands. At that time we need a consciousness that will go on knocking upon our closed eyes, ears and hearts with newer and newer versions of the new that will shred to pieces our frayed curtain and reveal the ever-new. How vast, how beautiful, how free this world is. What spirit, what light, what happiness! Man has encircled this world, observing it, contemplating it and constructing it in so many different ways. There is no limit to his spirit, his emotions and his imagination. This mind of man which encompasses the world has such endless and extraordinary diversity. All of them together comprise my world. That is why my heart hears within it a call to circumnavigate the world and see everything with my own eyes.

No one has the capacity or the opportunity to see through every nook and corner of this immense diversity exhaustively. If you just go out to see the universe then you can attain the fruits of your vision. Though in a sense the universe exists everywhere, one can sense it only if we leave our languor aside, do away with our habits, open our eyes and venture out. Only then the confinement in our vision is removed, our soul is reborn and we can savour the spirit of the universe. The person who lacks initiative and is immobile loses even the things that are right in front of him. So when we struggle to seek out the treasures near us we then manage to grasp it at a very profound level. The real intention of all our travels is this—whatever is there, things which cannot be lost have to be reaffirmed at every step by saying, 'It's there, it's there, it's there', touching the ancient things in newer and newer ways with all our heart.

Red Sea
Jaisthya 21, 1319 B.S.
[First published in *Tattwabodhini Patrika*,
Sravana issue, 1319 B.S.]

Chapter 6

The Form of Happiness

This morning I stood on the deck of the ship holding the railings. In between the light blue sky and the dark blue water of the ocean a mild breeze was blowing in from the western horizon. It soothed my forehead. My mind seemed to say, 'This is the blessing of the divine.'

The mind does not respond like this at all times. On many occasions we witness the outside beauty only externally—something that soothes our eyes but does not get absorbed inside. It is just like smelling the divine fruit without tasting it.

But when that beauty directly affects your inner heart then on that day we perceive Infinity. Then the whole mind sings out instantly, 'No, no, it is not only colour and smell; it is divine nectar and the worldwide stream of blessing.'

This unprecedented beauty between the sky and the ocean which is revealing itself layer after layer in the early morning light, where does it reside? Is it in the water? Is it in the wind? Who can bear this which is beyond all understanding?

This is happiness, this is blessing. Through ages and across countries this has soothed and captured the mind of innumerable creatures and it never ends. So many poets have composed poetry after coming into contact with it; so many artists have created their art; so many mothers' hearts have been filled with compassion; so many hearts of lovers have become excited with love. Penetrating the depths of boundaries this limitless nectar-fountain of eternity has been energizing man in so many different ways that there seems to be no end to it. I don't see an end to it. This is strange, really strange.

This is '*Anandaroopammritam*', the height of eternal happiness. Beauty is not the final word here, death is not the last meaning. It is happiness through beauty, eternity through death. What do we gain from being born on this earth if we are only stuck up with beauty or feel that all worries end with death? We have seen materialism and not truth.

Do I have only eyes and ears? Don't I have truth in me or happiness? When I see the world completely through my truth or happiness then I see this undulating ocean in front of me, this blowing breeze, this spread of light not as material things but as happiness, and all its meanings lie within Him. I hardly know what He is saying or showing. Where these millions of streams of happiness come and meet and from where in one great flow they flow back to His heart—if I am able to stand for a brief moment I would be able to understand the ulterior purpose of all this, see the ultimate result. If we consider this unimaginable power, this undefinable beauty, this infinite truth, this unending happiness to be only earth and water then it is a terrible failure, a colossal waste. No, no, this is His blessing, this is His revelation that is touching me, embracing me, playing the lyre in my heart, enlivening me, arousing me, beckoning my mind from different corners of the world, transposing my moments into eras of eternity; there is no end, only more and more and more; but He is one, only one, and He is the happy, eternal one. He is the deep, unlimited, unfragmented, silent, quiet and serious one—but many are the waves, many are the songs that resound!

Filling my heart, slaking my thirst
Give me more and more, and even more strength.
In your world, in your mansion,
Give me more and more, and even more space.
On these eyes of mine, O Lord,
Stream more and more, and even more light.
Filling the stops of my flute, with tune after tune,
O Lord, grant me more, and even more music.
Give me more, even more pain,
O Lord, give me the power to perceive.
Breaking doors, removing obstacles
Relieve me, O Lord; set me completely free!
In love, and even more love
Let the 'I' in me be fully subsumed.
Pouring nectar, confer yourself,
O Lord, give more, and even more of your self!

Red Sea
Jaisthya 22, 1319 B.S.
[First published in *Tattwabodhini Patrika, Sravana* issue, 1319 B.S.]

Chapter 7

Two Desires

It is only man who says that there is no end to hope. No other creature in the world says this. All the other creatures live within the limits of nature and all their desires are also restricted within those limits. Animals do not like to change their eating or roaming habits and they do not exceed their natural requirements. If they are satisfied at one place then they know where to stop. Their wishes end spontaneously as soon as their need is fulfilled; after that they do not have a second desire to again pursue and awaken that wish.

It is only in man's nature that we see one desire riding on the back of another one. After the stomach is full and when the desire to eat ends on its own, man is urged to keep alive that desire through another wish. By consuming pickle, by applying medicines, he overrides the weary desire to eat and moves beyond necessity.

This actually causes sufficient harm to man because this is not a natural desire. A natural desire easily remains confined and contented within its natural limits. And man's unnatural desire never feels satisfied. There is something in him which is forever saying—more, more, more!

But why does man have a desire which can harm him? Looking towards this indomitable desire man has imagined a Satan in the business of the world. In the Jewish epic when the first man and woman were in heaven then God had asked them to keep their desires within natural limits, by saying 'Remain satisfied within this. You remain within your natural world, don't try to enter the world of knowledge.' Every living creature in heaven remained restricted within the limits of that satisfaction; only man said, 'Whatever we have got, we want more.' This stepping towards the more is a very dangerous state. Here there are no limits for natural satisfaction and so there is no one to advice how far you can go in one direction. The threat of death in this state of dissatisfaction and directionlessness looms large. He who led man into such an uncontrollable situation was cursed by him and called Satan.

But whether we are angry or not, we cannot accept Satan in the world. It has to be admitted that this desire of man to have more is not an external attack by an enemy. Man can blame his senses for this, but this desire is really his human desire. So as long as he cannot conquer this desire, so long he shall never be at peace, he shall be hurt and will keep on going round and round.

But how does man conquer this desire for more? If he eats then his stomach will be full, if he enjoys then at one point it has to come and stop. The desire for 'more' then will have to come to a certain limit and get defeated. It is not just simply getting defeated; he will be sad and in that case also cause sadness. Diseases will come, unnaturalness will come and he will prevent himself as well as others. This is because where nature has drawn the limits, to cross that means punishment.

Not only that if we try to impose this desire for 'more' within the natural jurisdiction then we will fall down one upon the other. If we want more than what we have then we will have to approach and lay hands on what you have. Then we will either have to apply deceit or use open force to achieve it. This is when deceit by the weak and rampant intolerance by the strong upsets the whole society turning it upside down.

This is how sin and destruction comes. But if this sin never came then man would not be able to find his path. This dissatisfaction and longing for more would drag him along to the place where the burning fire of sin would remind him to control the horse and bring it back. That is why in this human world above other things that educate human beings is prevalent that arduous practice to bring that desire for more under control. This is because God has gifted man with this tremendous carriage—it is not certain where it will lead us to. You harness it and learn to drive it. But that doesn't mean we will stop its fodder completely and kill it. This is because this desire for more is man's real vehicle.

The desire to fulfil requirement is the vehicle of animals. If that was not there then their life would not move along. This desire is the basis of natural life. It is the desire to do away with sadness. Where this desire receives an obstruction there it creates sadness in animals; wherever it is fulfilled it brings joy to them. That is why we find happiness and sadness in animals but no sin or redemption.

But this desire for more in human beings is not a desire for comfort or happiness; in fact it is a desire for sorrow. That man doesn't bother about his own life and moves around to discover the North Pole and South Pole of knowledge, love and power, is not the longing for happiness. It is not a desire for fulfilling present needs.

Indeed, man has two levels of desires. Among them one is the desire for certain requirements and the other is unnecessary desire. One is something which is totally necessary and we cannot do without it; the other is something we can easily do without. Strangely enough this second category of desire is so strong in man's mind that when it arises it easily scatters and destroys the first desire. Then he does not bother to listen to any demand for happiness, ease or requirement. Then he says, 'I don't want happiness, I want the "more". This happiness is not my happiness, the "more" is my happiness.' Then he says, *Bhumaiva Sukham*, happiness is spread in the entire world.

This happiness is not what we understand as mere pleasure. This omnipresent happiness is not pleasure but a beatific delight. The difference between the two is that the opposite of happiness is sorrow but the opposite of delight is not sorrow. Just as Shiva had drunk poison, delight also accepts sorrow easily. So much so that it is through sorrow that delight becomes successful and realizes its completeness. So worshipping sorrow is the worship of ananda.

That is why I see that like all other animals the lower desire of man is to do away with his sorrow and the higher level of desire is to overcome sorrow and gain ananda. This desire is constantly telling us, *Nalpe Sukham asti, Bhumatweva Bijigyasitavya,* not to restrict our happiness within narrow limitations but to understand the greater world.

So in nature_the animal remains confined within its traditional limits and with its simple feelings tries to reduce sorrow. Man with his imagination did not want to remain confined within any limits of knowledge, love and power. He said, 'I don't want to abide by habits, traditions, rules. I want to know fulness.'

If that is true then what was the necessity of man's efforts to control this desire for more, this desire for ananda. If he had just shut his eyes to this tremendous desire and surrendered himself then his humanity would have been successful.

The main reason to control desire forcefully is that man has faced a great dilemma in order to ascertain the right of two desires. There is a particular field of our natural desires within which we are confined. There is danger if we forcibly try to stretch our desires beyond the natural limits. The limits of this fencing is to a certain extent static, so till a certain point it can withstand the pull. If we become daring and go on stretching that further then Ravana's golden palace of Lanka is destroyed, the Tower of Babylon falls down. If we go on winding the stick of churning towards the side of more then what comes up to the surface is disease, adversity and the poison of sin.

It is seen that the ego part of man is rather constricted. If you try to take in too much of anything there then that too becomes a burden. Trying to take your own happiness, your own interest and your own power to a limitless extent is like committing suicide. In that context one cannot carry the burden of the Supreme Being. God is repulsive in his eating and pleasure and self-interest.

For this reason when man's desire for more enters the area of his brittle ego like a mad elephant then he faces terrible danger. If that brought in sorrow for himself and for others only then it wouldn't be so bad. But its misery is worse than that. It brings in sin and it cannot be measured with sorrow. I have already mentioned, man is not only harmed by sorrow—in fact, sorrow can also be beneficial to man—but sin is man's greatest loss.

Yes, you can see the opposite side of this too. When man's required desires, that is, limited domestic desires leave selfish limits and try to enter the level of spiritual meditation, even that is very nasty. That is because then man only starts to keep account of all holy activities. Whatever is complete happiness, something that is beyond any result, they even start calculating, and multiplying and dividing that. And depending on that calculation man becomes proud, he gets entangled in external manifestations and keeps on hoarding his selfish and limited purity just like a miser. Then like an experienced householder, in the field of that Supreme Being, he makes a barrier and thus creates materialism. This is also another kind of sin. It externalizes spiritual values and creates meanness out of spiritualism.

This sinful feeling that appears in man's mind, if we give it a thought for the sake of description, then we see that that greatness of desire which takes us towards God, a pull towards the exact opposite of this path, that of the small ego, not only creates sorrow—in fact in some cases it might not even create sorrow—but we lose God for it. Our greatness, our truth is thus destroyed. This is no botheration for an animal but for man there is no destruction like it. The feeling of destruction does not affect everyone's spirit in the same way. In fact, for some it is very bleak. But overall in the human mind this feeling of sin is much larger than the feeling of sorrow. It is so large that man wants to condone this sin through plenty of sorrow. That man is expressing his deepest misfortune by using the word sin is proof enough that man is revealing his truest identity.

That identity is that man's natural terrain is not within a limited nature, his happiness is in infinity; the real truth is not towards the self but towards the universal one. The great desire that man has found within himself does not want to acknowledge littleness. Through severe austerities it is ceaselessly leading man towards blissful salvation in knowledge, science, art, literature. And with love, devotion and purity it is successfully pulling man's entire consciousness into a limitless and deep sea of nectar. Whatever impedes that movement of man towards that ultimate destination, draws him in the opposite direction that is sin, that is his destruction.

Red Sea

Jaisthya 23, 1319 B.S.

[First published in *Prabasi, Sravana* issue, 1319 B.S.]

Chapter 8

Inside and Outside

When I first woke up in my bed early in the morning and looked out of the cabin window I saw that there were waves in the ocean today. There was a strong westerly wind and as I lent my ears to listen to the sound of the waves; at one point of time I felt as if a song was being played in some hidden instrument. The sound of that song was not as strong as the thunder in the sky; it was deep and slow. Just as the singular tune of a violin affects the heart even above other loud-sounding percussion instruments, in a similar way the continuous flow of that slow and serious melody filling the heart of the sky was reverberating. In the end it so happened that the tune that I was hearing within my heart wanted to come out from the throat and I attempted that. But this kind of an attempt is an oppression and it destroys the peace of the larger tune and that is why I kept quiet.

One thing came to my mind. This song that occurred in my mind early in the morning was inspired by the ocean but it was not the echo of the sound of the wind or the waves. In no way could it be called an imitation of the water or the wind encircling the sky. It was totally independent; it was a song whose tunes were unfolding slowly like the opening up of the petals of a flower one by one.

But I was feeling that this was nothing independent. It was an integral part of the eternal sonorous rhythm of this great ocean. This song was like the fumes of the incense sticks in the puja temple, that after filling each little corner was spreading upwards towards the sky. Whatever was emanating from the breath of the ocean in its ardour, appeared as sound, but was its inner song.

There is a connection between the outside and the inside but it is not the connection of likeness; rather complete dissimilarity. Both are present there but where that link between the two is difficult to ascertain. It is an indescribable connection, not a link that can be directly proved.

The throbbing is hurting the eye and I am seeing light in my heart; some objects are touching the body and beauty is arising in the mind; events are taking place outside and happiness and sorrow are rising inside like the lilting of the waves. One has a shape and it can be analysed; the other does not have any shape and it is indivisible. What I understand to be 'me' is certain external sounds, smell and touch; a few moments of thoughts and emotions; but through all these things one thing that is expressing itself completely is 'me.' This 'me' is not just a replica of its external manifestation, instead its contrast with the exterior is expressing it aptly.

Artists and connoisseurs yearn to express this wonderful intrinsic aspect of the world. That is why their effort to express it through imitation can never be successful. On many occasions our thoughts become stagnant due to habit. Then we cannot see beyond what our eyes see. If we accept the visible form to be ultimate and believe in it then that inert identity does not arouse our mind. Then we move around, work but do not accept the world with our heart. This is because it is the internal beauty of the world which is the matter of the mind. It is the task of poets and connoisseurs to do away with the veil of habits and reveal that beauty.

This is why they do not imitate our traditional form but displace it. They take one form within another and dismiss its claim of being the ultimate. The visible things are made to take the place of audible ones and the audible ones are transformed into the orbit of visual things. In this way they have shown that beauty in this world is not eternal truth; it is a metaphor. Only if we can go inside that metaphor can we be freed from its chains; only then can we get relief through happiness.

Our experts created music in ragas Bhairo and Todi and said that they are to be sung in the morning. But do we get any resemblance to the different sounds of newly-awakened morning life in it? Not at all. Then what is the point in calling Bhairo and Todi morning ragas? This means that these connoisseurs have listened to all the sounds and silences of morning and have done it from their hearts. So it will be futile trying to match some external aspects of morning with this music.

I like this special quality of music in our country very much. In our country different ragas have been composed to welcome morning, noon, afternoon, evening, midnight, monsoon and spring. I do not know whether everyone will like all these ragas. At least I do not consider or feel in my heart raga Sarang to be an afternoon raga. Anyhow, the new ragas that play at different times in different seasons in the private music room in God's very own abode have entered our experts' ears. In our country the ragas Todi and Canara let us know that apart from the external manifestation there is a deeper internal expression as well.

The big music composers in Europe must have tried some way or the other to express the internal message of the world through their songs. If we get to know their compositions well then we can discuss about these issues. At present as an outsider in the crowd trying to listen to a European music concert I have a few things coming to my mind.

A few passengers of our ship sometimes play music and sing songs in the evening. Whenever such an occasion takes place I too go and sit in the corner of that room. It is not that I like English songs and that is what draws me towards it. But I know for sure that there is a devotion in liking good things. That which fascinates us, without devotion, is only a false illusion and what discourages it is really delightful. That is why I practise listening to European songs. Even when I don't like it, I don't dismiss it with disrespect.

There is a young man and one or two ladies in this ship who more or less sing well. I can see, the audience express special happiness for their songs. On the days the concert becomes lively one song after another is sung. Some songs praise England, some are sad farewell songs of the depressed lover and some offer love by the lover. I have noticed something special in all of them. Both the tune of the song and the singer's voice emphasize the quality of loudness. That emphasis is not the inner strength of that music, it seems more of an external manifestation. In other words, it is an attempt to highlight the rise and fall of emotions with tune and voice.

This is natural. Depending upon the exuberance of emotions the volume of our speech is sometimes very soft and sometimes very loud. But songs are not to imitate habits, because songs and acting are not the same thing. If we add acting to songs then the pure power of songs gets covered up. That is why when I sit in the saloon of the ship and listen to their songs, then I am constantly reminded of the fact that the singers here are trying to push the feelings of the heart too hard and trying to point them out through their fingers.

But we really don't want to see music from external angles. It is not my concern to know exactly what or how the lover is feeling. We want to know what is internally playing within the emotions. This external expression and internal expression of emotions are of totally different kinds. Because what is emotion externally is beauty internally. This too is independent just as the frequency of ether and the expression of light are totally independent.

We shed tears when we cry and laugh when we are happy and that is natural. But if the singer of a sad song combines laughter with tears, then we are insulting the goddess of music. In reality when tears from inside do not fall out and the laughter within does not resound, it is then that music can be said to have made its impact. There through human laughter and tears man's sensibility is dispersed into the Infinity where the song of all trees, plants, rivers and fountains expresses itself through our happiness and desires. We can understand the bytes in our heart to be one with the universe.

But we create impediments in the depth of that music when we put too much emphasis on tune and voice and try to imitate the feelings of our heart. Music has a natural rise and fall similar to the tide of the ocean but it is entirely its own. Like poetic rhythm this rise and fall of music is the dance-steps, the throw of her dance-steps, and not the instrument of our emotions like a puppet play.

Though acting depends on imitation more than other arts, nevertheless it is not just following the professional mimic like the Harbola. It has also taken up the responsibility of opening up the normal curtain and showing us what is inside. If you tend to emphasize too much on naturalism then the inside gets blurred. It is often seen on stage that in order to show the greatness of human emotions the actors forcefully highlight their voice delivery and gestures. The reason for this is that the person who does not express the truth but tries to imitate it exaggerates things in the way a false witness does in court. He does not have the courage to exercise control. In the theatre stages of our country we see the display of such exaggerated acting every day. But I saw the greatest example of that in England. There I had gone to watch the performance of *Hamlet* and *The Bride of Lamarmoor* by the famous actor Irving. I was totally puzzled after watching the powerful acting of Irving. I had never seen such uncontrolled and exaggerated acting that totally destroys the clarity of the subject. It only rocks us from the outside and prevents us from going into the depth of the situation.

Apart from anything else, art requires control. This is because control is the gateway to enter inside. Those people who want to gain spiritual truth also reduce external manifestations and focus on control. That is why a strange thing is being said about gaining spirituality and that is '*Tyaktena Bhunjitha*', to enjoy by sacrificing. The utmost dedication of art is also the worship of the Supreme Being. That is why the true business of art is not to sway the heart by force. Its true mission is to go within the depth of ourselves through self-control. One should not imitate whatever one sees in front of one's eyes; or one should not use broad brush strokes and exaggerate it so much that it becomes mere child's play.

Usually European art tries to impress upon us by pushing hard and forcing things upon our heart. Europe actually wants to see reality as it should be seen. That is why whenever I see a devotional picture we see the external manifestation of piety as folded palms, the head raised towards the sky, with the eyeballs turned upside down. Those students in our country who want to imitate English art follow this procedure of imitation of manner. They think that if they emphasize upon reality then their work of art is done properly. That is why when they have to draw the picture of Narada, they go and draw the picture of the artist who plays Narada in the folk theatre form of *jatra*, because they do not have the power to imagine him through meditation; in fact they have never seen Narada except in a *jatra* performance.

In the Buddhist era of our country, the Greek artists had sculpted the ascetic statue of Buddha. His starving skeletal figure was ideally replicated; one could literally count the ribs on his body. The Indian sculptors had also sculpted the ascetic statue of Buddha but their work does not show the real history of starvation or fasting. There was no account of the ribs and bones in that statue; it was not required to take a medical certificate. Because it did not bother to account for reality, it could express the truth. The businessman artist is a witness of the present, and the true artist is witness to truth. We can see reality through our eyes, but truth can only be seen through the mind. If we want to see with the mind then we have to neglect the things we see through our eyes. We have to tell the external beauty with courage, 'You are not the final, the ultimate; you are not the target but a simple means to the end.'

Arabian Sea

Jaisthya 25, 1319 B.S.

[First published in *Bharati*, *Sravana* issue, 1319 B.S.]

Chapter 9

Play and Work

Port Said is the first port in the Mediterranean Sea. From here we have to begin our journey to Europe. We reached the harbour in the evening. Lights from the city were already glowing from the windows. A whole lot of small rowing boats and motor boats have crowded around our ship in order to take the passengers to the shore. Here many people disembarked to go around the shops and markets in Port Said. I did not get down in that crowd. Holding the railing of the ship I stood watching everything. The place where the dark sea meets the dark sky, man has lit up a little space there with a few lights of his own and has totally denied the presence of the night.

Several new passengers are supposed to join us at Port Said. The earlier group is very annoyed upon hearing this news. Man is happy to discover new things, but they grow tense when they hear about new people. As soon as they come by, he has to develop both an internal as well as an external understanding with him. And this is not only a matter of curiosity. He nudges many other people with his heart. There is no other crowd than the crowd of men.

Most of the people who boarded the ship at Port Said were French. Our deck is full of people and one has to be an excellent rowman to sail through this crowd of human-boats without touching one another.

I have already watched several times how the European men and women spend their days on the deck from morning till ten o'clock at night and am watching it again. The first thing you notice is that they are always restless and we are not used to such restlessness. In our warm country we always prefer to remain cool and so we start feeling hot even if someone acts restless in front of our eyes. The disciplines in our country are—'Keep quiet', 'Stay calm', 'Don't increase your work unnecessarily.' Here these people always say, 'Let's do something'. That is why all these old and young people are always jumping around. There is no end to the way they laugh, chat, play and enjoy themselves.

Removing the obstacle of habit when I look at this scene then I feel that I am watching an external manifestation of nature. It seems as if a waterfall is gushing down, a river is flowing and the trees are all shaking in the wind. They are unable to spend all their vitality in spite of performing all the required functions and are expressing themselves on their own through the abundance of that remaining energy instead.

When we go somewhere with a small child then we make a provision for some toys, otherwise it becomes very difficult for the child to remain quiet. This is because the flow of energy is always in excess of the amount required by him. If he does not have the necessary things to entertain himself he gets agitated as he cannot spend that bubbling energy. This is why small children run around unnecessarily. Their shouts have no meaning, their games make some knowledgeable people laugh, whereas some also feel irritated. But however much their playfulness might irritate us, there is no doubt that it becomes much more troublesome if you try and stop those games.

Countless number of games have been arranged for all these European passengers who have boarded the ship. If we owned the ship then we would be happy to provide quiet games like cards or dice and would not encourage any of these physically active games. At least for the few days of our journey we would especially discard these unnecessary burdens and nobody would also mind it. But these European passengers need games to keep themselves calm. Even the daily activities are not enough to pacify all the extra energy that is stored up in their bodies. In order to remain quiet they have to be kept constantly occupied and have to be supplied with innumerable toys and games.

This is why I see these young and old people are always fidgety and enjoying themselves. Since this seems totally unnecessary to us, it appears quite strange in the beginning. I keep on thinking that such childishness on the part of aged people is simply a lack of restraint. Because childhood is a time for playing games it suits them well but at an age when one should work, such excitement for playing games is totally unwarranted.

But when I see that such exuberance and excitement for games is just natural behaviour for these Europeans, then I see a beauty in the whole affair. It seems somewhat like the unnecessary exuberance of spring when there are more buds than what would actually blossom into fruits. But if this unnecessary exuberance was not there then there would be a dearth of the necessary items at every step.

There is nothing to be ashamed of the games that they play. This is because these games are not meant for idle people to while away their time. We have seen that the energy in their hearts is not expended only in playing. The effect of this endless energy is found in their tireless enterprise, unhindered influence at workplace too. If we think about the efficiency with which they have been able to spread their working nets then we are just stunned. So much unlimited physical and mental endeavour is embedded within it. There is no stagnation, no laxity; they are always alert and never waste the least bit of opportunity.

The same energy that keeps a person always active in work also functions during their relaxation and play. I cannot just dismiss this profusion of energy like an all-knowing person. It is actually spreading the wealth of man in newer creations. They are giving up parts of themselves in different directions and so are getting that back in return several times more. It is this energy that is not ready to accept any limit in building empires, in trade, science, literature and is constantly knocking hard at the closed door of the weak.

This strength of enterprise, of which games forms one side and work another, is truly beautiful. When in a woman we see a reflection of Goddess Lakshmi, we see on one hand dressing up and dalliance, and capability of endless work and skill in serving others on the other. The split between these two attributes is ugly. In reality, strength expresses itself through beauty, and the lack of it results in laxity and mismanagement which gradually sucks one down in the morass of ugliness. Ugliness is the enemy of the people; it is where ill health, poverty and blind superstition resides. This is where man resigns himself to fate and states, 'I have lost hope and have left everything to fate'. This is where there is a split between the two; the work that is begun never ends and whatever one wants to build up breaks down. Lack of strength is the real ugliness.

This is actually what I see amidst all their fun and frolic on the deck. There is a sort of discipline that comes out naturally through all their games. That is why there is no chaos or indiscipline even in their play or entertainment. Everyone wears proper clothes as and when required. There is also a sort of discipline in the way they acquaint themselves with each other and no one can cross those limits. Because everything is so disciplined their exuberance in games and entertainment can be performed with such a tremendous force without causing any disaster.

I cannot help but imagine a scene where no one else but people from our country have assembled here upon the deck. At the very outset we would have seen that no single arrangement would have worked between two people. Our habits and behaviour do not let us work amicably with one another. There is a space among the Europeans where they are independent and there is another one where they belong to everybody. Where they are independent it is their private space and it is very clearly demarcated. No one has open access there and everyone abides by that norm. They spend their personal lives there according to their own wishes and habits in that space. But whenever they come out of that they surrender themselves to everyone's rules and do not drag in their private lives at any cost. Because these two divisions are clearly demarcated, the interaction with others becomes easy and organized for them. But since we do not have such divisions among us everything goes haywire and no one wants to maintain any limitations. If we had this deck then we would use it according to our own requirements. We would have left our bundles scattered here and there. Some of us would be brushing our teeth, some would lay out a bed by blocking the path and sleep on it, some would smoke the hookah and then throw the ashes and the burnt tobacco everywhere. Also some would get their servants to massage their bodies with oil and do it with a lot of fanfare. Different utensils would be just lying scattered here and there and there would be no end to the shouts and calls. If anyone would try to bring in some sort of discipline within this chaos we would feel terribly insulted resulting in great annoyance and repeated anger. Also no one would be least bit worried that the other person might want to read or write or do some other work or that he too would occasionally want to relax. It would suddenly be found that somebody has pulled away and started reading the book I was reading; my binoculars would be passed around different people and no one would bother to return it to me. Someone would casually pick up my notebook from my table and start looking at it; others would drop in uninvited and start gossiping; some enthusiastic person might start singing in a loud voice without considering whether it was the appropriate time or space and without being shy about the lack of sweetness in his voice. If anything was lying somewhere then it would simply remain like that. If someone was eating a fruit then he would scatter its peel and seeds on the deck and the entire day would be spent in searching a thousand times for misplaced utensils, shawls, socks, comforters.

This would not only create discomfort on both sides; in fact happiness, comfort and beauty would disappear from all sides. Let alone work, it would also prevent fun and enjoyment. The power that succeeds in maintaining discipline in work also helps to retain the same discipline in our fun and enjoyment and makes it beautiful and enjoyable. As the soldier naturally wears his sword a strong person naturally and lovingly likes to maintain discipline. This is his weapon and if the strong does not abide by discipline it fails itself.

When a powerful person maintains discipline then he doesn't do it just to abide by the law but does it to satisfy himself. And when the weak obeys the rules then he does it either out of fear or out of greed or simply out of sheer mechanical habit. He kneels down before the rules and abides by it. But when he is not bound to obey, but has to do it only for himself, then it is weakness which makes him evade rules and by doing so he evades himself. It is there where all his ugliness and intemperance lies.

Man has not respected man's strength of freedom wherever he has been ruled by external forces. Whenever the king or the guru and the scriptures have forced him to seek welfare without any logic, there he has ignored rules doused in the happiness of his own strength. If man gets used to working only by force then he will not work whenever he is set free. This is why whenever we obey the rules we obey them like slaves and when we don't obey them, we evade them like slaves. That is why when our society was ruled by rules then water was available in the water bodies, education is the schools and shelter in the roadside inns. When the external control of society has become lax, we do not have roads, ghats, or water in the lakes and ponds. People no longer have the natural energy to help others, or to tide over these drawbacks and work for the welfare of man. We keep on either blaming our fate or look up expectantly towards the government.

But among these it is very difficult to make a distinction between work and its causes. Those who wear external rules freely as chains, later those external rules tie them up in chains. But those who have the indomitable power not to follow those rules blindly, they are the ones who can create new rules for the benefit of one's own happiness. Otherwise this right cannot be enjoyed even if it is just handed over to us. Independence is not an external manifestation but internal and so it is not possible to get it from someone by simply asking for it. Until we attain that independence through our own natural power, we shall be ruled upon, external discipline making us wear blinkers around our eyes and noose around our necks. Till that time, whatever we may say, we will want to keep on enforcing rules and regulations upon others whenever we get the opportunity. When we want sovereignty we will go on mouthing European history but in the social and domestic affairs the eldest will go on imposing upon the youngest and the strong person will curb the rights of the weak. If we want to commit ourselves to the welfare of another person then we like that to be done as per our own thoughts and rules; we dare not let him become good according to his own standards. This is how we go on nurturing weakness within ourselves and at the same time want to gain the rights of the strong person externally like a god-sent gift received through dreams.

This is why I am very hurt to see that whenever we have got together to do some work or wherever we have gone to run an establishment by implementing our own rules, there we have become divisive and lax and therefore gradually destroyed everything. Our only problem is not to save ourselves from any external enemy but from our own internal weakness and lack of aesthetics. We have to say this with total determination that the rules that can be worn as a garland around the neck should not be worn as a chain on our feet. It has to be clearly understood that we have to abide by the truth. When we accept that truth from within our hearts then we are happy but when we simply follow it externally then we are sorrowful. When there is lack of power to accept the truth within ourselves it is then that the control becomes severe on the outside; then we should not chide the external world to keep ourselves free of guilt.

[First published in *Tattwabodhini Patrika,*
Bhadra issue, 1319 B.S.]

Chapter 10

In London

The ocean trip was over. Over the last two days there were fierce winds; that upsurge in the ocean resulted in a kind of parallel internal disturbance within us. I thought about it and decided that the ocean was not to blame for it; it was the captain's fault. We reached two days after the scheduled date of arrival. Varuna, the lord of the winds, surely had arranged his quota of storms and wind beforehand for this weak traveller; but human calculations proved incorrect.

Running from Marseilles to Paris, I was relieved for a day. Cleaning the salt of the ocean from the body, I surrendered myself to the land. After food and drinks, I made a quick round of the streets of Paris in a motor car.

Seen from the outside, Paris seems to be the playground of the whole of Europe. Here the lights of the playhouses never go off. There are arrangements for entertainment everywhere. The beautiful city of Paris has dressed up such a lot only to please man. I just keep on thinking that she does not make an effort to please man easily.

When the whole world was ruled by kings, then feasts and entertainment would take place in an enormous scale in the king's palace. Now every man is a king. This pleasure house for all men is a huge affair. There is no limit as to how many slaves are working for it day and night. One hardly keeps a track of how many shiploads and trainloads of materials arrive everyday from distant countries of the world for this purpose alone.

This entertainment industry for the man-king is growing so varied in nature that I do not feel like comparing it with the fun and enjoyment created for the lazy pleasure-seekers. It is great entertainment with great human zeal; an impossible effort to please someone who is not easily satisfied. Many people have sunk in the vortex of enjoyment, some while enjoying the pleasure and some while striving to supply them. But even then, in general, one can see through it the image of human power and victory that cannot be ignored.

On Sunday we crossed the ocean from Calais and reached Dover. I felt a great sense of comfort when I boarded the train along with other English passengers. It seemed as if I had arrived among my relatives. This is because I know the language of the English. The language of man is like a stream of light. The further this language spreads the more man expresses his inward feelings on his own. Along with the English language, I have acquired the English heart. Whatever I get to know gives pleasure. In France I had gained knowledge through the eyes, but was deprived of knowledge of the heart. That is why there was a denial of pleasure. As soon as I stepped into Dover I felt that the deprivation was gone. It was not that I was just standing on the ground, the soil, but that I had entered the heart of man.

I've come to London after a long time. The streets of London were crowded then also, but now the motor car was an added element. It has made the bustling nature of the city even more visible. Motor cars of all kinds—motor buses and carry trucks were running in a hundred directions on the arterial roads of London. I keep on thinking about the tremendous forcefulness of this movement through the streets of London. How great was the mental force whose external manifestation this was! How fiercely they were tugging at time and space. The pedestrians were becoming more cautious each day. Whatever thoughts they might have in their minds, each day they also had to simultaneously adjust themselves with these strange external movements. Miscalculation could be dangerous. Just as the faculties of the deer become extra-sensory when it comes to saving himself from the attack of violent animals, similarly the sensibilities of the human beings here are sharpened extraordinarily under the pressure of hurried movement everywhere. They were gaining the strength to decide about the right course of action through quick sight, quick listening and quick thought. Those who took time to watch and think would have to retreat to the back here.

I am gradually meeting my friends. Because the care and love I was receiving was from foreign hands, it seemed doubly valuable to me; the idea of how close one man was to another could be understood more intimately through distance.

I had in the meantime been invited to lunch by the *Nation*, which is the main weekly newspaper of the liberals here. The *Nation* has been the mouthpiece of the ideas and speeches of all the great English thinkers who do not weigh people in the false scale of selfishness both in their own country and abroad, their own race and others; those who do not support injustice at any pretext; those who are real friends of all mankind.

The editor and the contributors of *Nation* assemble once a week for lunch to discuss different issues. Later they also chalk out the modalities of the articles for the following week. It need not be said that all the contributors to this first-class newspaper are efficient and erudite men. I was very happy to be part of their lunch meet and discussions on that day.

Sitting among them I realized that each of them was aware of his true responsibility towards society. They not only composed sentences, but each of their articles swayed the boat of British imperialism either right or left. In such a situation the writer cannot but immerse his whole self in his writing. There is no such necessity for newspapers in our country; we do not claim any responsibility from our writers and for this reason they are lazy, do not exert their total power and finish their work without seriousness. This is also why our editors do not feel the necessity for the education and awareness of our authors; the readers just accept whatever the authors write without protest. Because we are not cultivating in the field of truth, the harvest part in our sprout is very frugal—the food for the mind is not completely taking birth.

In political and other meetings in our country, I have seen that the voice is much louder than words. But the debates conducted here are held peacefully and with deep understanding. Instead of putting impediments, the difference of opinion actually enhanced the subject of discussion. I understood quickly how they have learnt the easy method of working together. They do important work but the manner of pursuing it does not encourage unnecessary conflict or waste. Their vehicle is huge and fast-paced also; but its wheels rotate smoothly without creating any noise at all.

[First published in *Prabasi, Bhadra* issue, 1319 B.S.]

Chapter 11

Friend

After coming to London I put up in a hotel. It seemed as if I had arrived at the corridors of habitation where men keep on going and coming. I don't know what is happening inside, I am not informed about it and don't make acquaintances with any person. I only watch people going and coming. I realize this much that there is no limit to their business, but I don't understand why they need to be so much like this. I do not know where this tremendous hurry goes and hits itself; whether it is harming or improving them and whether anyone is keeping record of it. The bell rings ding dong and going to the dining hall I find two or three men and women sitting around small tables and eating their food in silence. The tall steward with a serious face is moving around swiftly and serving all the people; some are reading newspapers while having their meals, and after opening their watch and quickly glancing at it to check the time, wear their hats and walk out of the room speedily. The room becomes empty. Some people get together a few times during their meals and then no one knows where each one goes. I do not have the necessity but I too follow the others and open my watch several times and then close it again to put it back in my pocket. When it is neither time for the meals nor time to sleep, then the hotel seems like a boat tied to the land—if you have to stay there at that time you do not find any explanation for it. Those who do not have a place to live but only a place to work, for them, a hotel suits the best. Those who are essentially unnecessary people like me, for them living in this mass housing style is not worth it. Upon opening the window I find streams of people moving in all directions. I imagine that they are like hammers belonging to an invisible craftsman. What is being built up is also more or less invisible; it is a big factory of history; millions of hammers are being hit at great speed at millions of places. I stand outside that engine and watch the live hammers powered by the steam of hunger running about at an indomitable speed.

Whenever foreigners come here for the first time they notice this extremely huge human factory which the god of history has created. What power, what sound, what rolling of wheels! I try to close my eyes and think about the tremendous perseverance in this entire movement and work in London. Where is this incessant force heading and towards what goal is it hitting? What is that unspoken thing which it is stirring up for expression!

But the days cannot be spent by just looking at this mechanical side of man. If I could not get to know his human identity, then why did I come? But it is easier to see man as a machine, rather than man as a human being. If the man inside does not come on his own and call you then you cannot enter his heart. But that is not like just going and buying a theatre ticket. It is a priceless thing that comes free of cost.

Fortunately, I got an opportunity—I met a friend. Just as a rose is a special type of flower among all the other flowers in the garden, a friend is also a special class of human being. There are some people who have been born on this earth just to become friends. They have unusual and natural power to give company to man. All of us love someone or the other in the world but even though we can love, all of us do not have the power to become friends. To become a friend you have to give company. Like other gifts, this gift also needs a treasury, because only desire isn't enough. Just as gems radiate with a natural glow, so also friendship radiates from the lives of few especially powerful people. This companionship that springs so naturally in love, goodwill, service, good-wishes and a merciful inner vision is a rare attribute. Just as a poet expresses his own happiness through language, so also people who are friendly by nature express their happiness through the daily lives of man.

The friend that I have found here has both the unlimited attributes of feeling happy as well as imparting happiness to others. The advantage of winning this sort of a friendly person is that one such person is equal to many friends. This is because such people consider having a human being who is close to your heart as the most important savings in their lives.

He is a famous painter and had been to India for a few days just some time ago. During that short time he had seen the heart of India. Feeling through the heart is almost like seeing through your eyes—it is not a matter of analysis, so it does not take much time. In India so many blind people are spending their entire lives without having that inner vision; they fail to see the light of our country which would enable them to see everything else quite clearly. Those who possess that necessary vision, their knowledge of another, even if for a brief period of time, is much more powerful than a blind man who knows another for a lifetime.

I had met him in India for a very brief period of time. His warmth of heart expressed itself so easily that my mind was instantly attracted towards him in a special way. The first thing that lured me in my journey to Europe was that I would be able to get closely acquainted with him.

As soon as I met him, I crossed the entrance of the hotel in a moment—there was no one to withhold me. Whenever there is a big crowd watching a live performance, a father lifts up his small child on his shoulders so that he can have a better sight. In a similar way the city of London has left one or two such high places above her shoulders for those citizens who want to look further above the heads of this crowd. Hampstead Heath in London is a sort of hilly region. It seems as if London has lifted herself up here. This region is part of the stone heart of the city which is still young and green and amidst the terrible office rush. This place is one where one can sit alone near the window of the open sky.

There is a small piece of garden on the hilly slope behind my friend's house. That little garden is filled up with the beauty of flowers like the palms of a small child. There is a long veranda adjacent to their drawing room which faces that garden and it is partly covered by delighted rose creepers full of innumerable bouquets of flowers. Whenever I wish I come and sit in this veranda with a book in my hand, and after that I don't feel the necessity of reading that book. The youthful exuberance and joy of his children—two small boys and a girl—is something I love to watch. I find a great difference between them and the children of our country. I feel as if we belong to an ancient age and somehow the children of our country also arrive in this world carrying the burden of that ancient tradition upon their back. They are good souls, their movements are restricted and their big and dark eyes are very pitiable. They do not ask too many questions and they try to find those answers on their own. These children here have been born in this world in a new age; they are exuberant with the youthfulness of life; they have to think and act diligently in all places. This is why they tend to run everywhere with their hurried feet and also place their hurried hands on everything. There is no doubt that the children in our country possess a natural frivolity but at the same time the gravitational force of stability always makes them a lot more inactive. These children do not have that invisible burden and so their lives are as sparkling as the dancing and gurgling waters of a fresh waterfall.

The wife of my friend is also very friendly. She has to perform the duties of a wife to the whole host of friends that her husband has. She has to look after them, nurture the beautiful relationships in every manner, take care of them when they are sick or comfort them when in sorrow, and all these form an important part of her domestic duties. This is not like doing her duties towards her relatives but a kinship with the circle of friends. The seat which is at the heart of this huge network is occupied by this devoted wife and never left vacant in this country.

I have mentioned earlier that my friend has a basically friendly nature and his talent for making friends is unparalleled. He has to select his friends very judiciously because he considers friendship akin to truth. A man who is not a true artist just draws anything and frames it up to decorate the empty walls of his house. But the true artist, for whom painting is an expression of truth, cannot obviously fill up his room with bad pictures. He selects the good pictures according to his discretion and natural judgment. This person also has not inflicted himself by getting acquainted with people according to social norms. All those who are in touch with him are his friends and all of them are talented and equally competent to be accepted as his friend.

Thus it is worthwhile mentioning that the person who is capable of having such renowned friends all around him definitely has some special virtues. He recognizes talent. Just as a bee hunts out the secret route to the nectar inside a flower and enters it easily, he too can do the same. He can undoubtedly select the good things and hold on to them. Many people are scared to express their true likings and speak only good things fearing that if they make a mistake then they would be humiliated. That is why whenever they have to welcome good things they always fall behind others. But this person does not have to fear that because he has a real conviction behind his own feelings. This is how he not only knows how to suck the nectar from the flower but also has the ability to love the flower as well. He is not a consumer but a lover. This is why he accepts as well as donates.

The path of acquaintance is much longer than that of unacquaintance. I did not have that much of time to cross that difficult path. Also I have little strength. Since I am forever in the habit of remaining in the sidelines I cannot even attempt to force myself amidst the crowd to reach my desired place. Moreover I do not have the key to the main door of the English language. So I always have to jump across the fences. It is difficult to move in that manner as you cannot retain your own nature or walk in a natural way. If you don't have the capability of getting yourself known to others then it is impossible to know the other person easily. So after getting tired of trying to save myself from the huge wheels of the monstrous motor cars here, I would at last go back to my own Bengal landscape, a land that is enfolded by so many rivers and is located next to the paddy fields glowing in the autumn sun. At this juncture my friend entered the scene and lifted the curtain. I saw that the seat has been laid and the lights were burning. Discarding the huge burden of being an unknown foreigner and shedding the dirty garb of a traveller, I moved from the crowd and entered a private space within a moment.

[First published in *Bharati, Kartik* issue, 1319 B.S.]

Chapter 12

The Poet Yeats

The poet Yeats is never lost in the crowd; he can be recognized as someone special. Just as his tall frame reaches above almost everyone else, so also whenever you see him you feel that he has an exuberance in all matters. It seems as if the Creator has created him like a gushing fountain with a tremendous urge to swell up from the level ground all around. That is why in his body, mind and spirit he seems to be many people all at once.

When I read the poetry of the contemporary poets in England, then I feel that they are not poets of the universe. They are just poets of the literary world. Poetry is being written in this country for quite a long time and so a lot of poetic language, style and metaphors have gradually accumulated. In the end it has become such a phenomenon that a person need not go to the basic fundamentals of poetic sources in order to write poetry. The poets have become like the ustads; that is, the necessity to sing from the core of the heart has disappeared; songs spring up from other songs. When only words come out of words and not out of pain, then the embellishments of words gradually become more and more complicated and fine because feelings apparently and deeply do not directly emanate from the recesses of the heart and are not simple. Because it doesn't trust itself it forcefully runs towards excesses; because contemporaneity doesn't come easily, it has to go looking for strange things to prove its excellence.

It will be easier to understand what I am implying if we compare Wordsworth with Swinburne. The latter is leading among the poets who are not poets of the world but are just poets for the sake of poetry. He has such exceptional skill in the mastery of words that he basks in its happiness. By stringing together words and rhymes in different ways he has painted very gaudy and colourful pictures but his place in the world is not one of wide expanse.

The direct conflict between the world and the heart has come out in the lyric poetry of Wordsworth. That is why it is so simple. It is not simple because it is easy. The readers do not accept it easily. When a poet composes poetry from direct feelings then that expresses itself completely naturally like flowers or fruits on the trees. It doesn't offer any explanations, nor does it force itself to make it more pleasant or close to the heart. It appears actually as it is and it is the reader's interest to accept and enjoy it.

Some people are born without the necessity of creating any difference between their own emotions and the subject of their emotions. They are able to express the essence of the world and human lives undoubtedly and with faith through the feelings of their heart. It is they who can only transcend all the artificiality of contemporary poetry with courage.

Once upon a time Burns was born during this period of artificiality in English poetry. He had experienced everything through his heart and expressed it accordingly. That is why the unbound Scottish heart could transcend the barrier of fixed formalities and undoubtedly create a place for itself in the world of poetry.

That the poet Yeats is much appreciated in the contemporary scenario of poetic literature is also for the same reason. Instead of echoing the contemporary poetry of his times, the poet has expressed the feelings of his own heart. Here one must understand what I mean by 'own heart'. Just as a piece of diamond expresses itself by reflecting the light from the sky, in a similar way a man's heart is not expressed through his own entity because there it is dark. When it can reflect something much larger than itself, only then it expresses itself in that light and also radiates that light. The heart of Ireland has come out through Yeats's poetry.

I should explain these words a bit more clearly. The rays of the same sun falls upon different clouds but the different colours that are reflected depend on the condition and the position of those clouds. But these different colours are not against one another; they can blend with the others through their individual varieties. However much one tries, coloured cotton wool can never imitate the colour of the clouds.

In a similar way either in Ireland, Scotland, or any other country, this radiance of the world falls upon the heart of its inhabitants in such a manner that it creates a special colour. This is how the world of man is becoming beautiful through such varieties of colour.

The poet not only expresses his own emotions, he also beautifully expresses the colours of the inner being of the country in which he resides. I am not saying that everyone can do it, but the person who can is blessed. The *Vaishnava Padavali* in our country is world poetry in its identity as 'Bengali poetry'. It is giving universal things to the world but along with it, it is adding a particular flavour that is entirely its own; in a container of beauty that is absolutely its own.

Those whose profession is to fight in the battlefield of the world, they have to armour and cover themselves with all kinds of cover and veil that society proffers otherwise they can be injured. But those who work to express themselves wholly, their lack of any covering is the real dress. I thought of all these things when I met the poet Yeats. Here was one person who was embracing the entire world with his unending sense of touch. This way of seeing all around is different from the way man sees everything through different kinds of learning, through practice or through imitation.

Whenever any person sees the world in this way unseen before and tells us about it, then we see that there is a similarity with man's earlier experience; it is not out of sync. Those who have seen through innocent eyes have seen it in this manner. Even the poets of the Vedic age have seen in land and water the presence of life, the presence of heart. To them the river, clouds, dawn, fire and thunderstorm did not reveal themselves as scientific truth; they unravelled themselves to the poet in the form the poets wished to see them in. The experiences of sorrow and happiness that is expressed in man's life seem to cover the entire earth and sky in wonderful disguises. As it is in our hearts so it is in our entire nature. Just as our little hearts are filled with laughter and sorrow, the pain of our longings and losses, in a similar way the same play is enacted in a massive scale in the stage of light and darkness spread across the universe. We cannot see it all together because it is so huge—we see it as water and we see it as earth, but do not see the huge game being played in the universe. But when man does not see through the blinkers of education and habit and sees through his entire mind, heart and life instead, then he sees a sort of suffering everywhere and realizes that it can only be expressed either through stories or through idioms. When man realized himself in a big way through all material things of the world, he understood in a certain way that what is not there in the whole world is also not within himself and what is there within himself is found in a greater way in the world. He could see this through the poet's vision—that is the vision of the heart and the vision of life and not the simple vision of the eyeball, the nerves and the brain. Its truth was not factual but emotional and it was painful. The language was also like that; it was musical language, the language of beauty. This language is the oldest language of human literature. But even now whenever a poet tries to realize the world through his suffering, then we find a similarity with his language and the ancient language of man. That is why epic stories of human beings are of no use in the scientific era—it only doesn't grow old in the poet's usage. Man's new realization of the world has made its way through that story and left its footprints there. Wherever the heart is awakened by this newness of realization there one sees the urge to travel to the older path.

The poet Yeats has channelled his poetry through that old fabular tradition. Since it was very natural for him it was through this tradition that he was able to attain such unprecedented fame. He is touching this world with his own life; not through his eyes or knowledge. That is why he does not see the world only in a materialistic way, he ascends to such lofty heights and experiences such a spirituality that is only accessible through meditation. If you have to express that through the process used in contemporary literature then you lose the essence and spirit of it because modernism in reality is not a new thing and has become impoverished with usage; it does not respond everywhere; it is like the dying embers. This fire is older than the ashes but it is young; the ashes are also modern but it is the old and wearied part. This is why everywhere poetry tries to sideline modern language and move on its own.

Everyone is aware that for some time now Ireland is going through the pangs of an awakening of the nationalistic spirit. This pain has become so great because English administration had been constricting the Irish spirit in every way. For a long time this pain has attempted to take the form of a political revolt. Ultimately along with that another attempt was also linked. Ireland felt the freedom of its soul and decided to express it.

In this context I am being reminded of our own country. For quite some time in our country too there was a serious attempt by the educated people to gain political power. It is seen that most of the leaders who attempted this did not have any contact with the literature or customs and practices of the country. They also had hardly any contact with the ordinary people. Whatever they needed to do for the development of the country they did it in the English language and with the help of the English government. They did not pay attention to the fact that the ordinary people of the country should also be involved in it.

But fortunately, in Bengal, we had begun to feel our hearts through literature. The main achievement of Bankimchandra is that he brought in such an era in Bengali literature when the Bengalis could find happiness and pride in being able to speak about themselves in their own language. Before that we were school children; we would combine the dictionary and grammar to write the exercises in the English school and we would neglect our own language and literature. But with the sudden appearance of *Bangadarshan*, we saw a certain power and ability within ourselves. We realized that we too had a literature that could really satisfy our mental hunger. This was the beginning and it did not end there. Before that we had kept our eyes closed and said that we had nothing, now we started looking for all the things we had. Those who had placed Kant and Mill on the throne during the beginning of *Bangadarshan*, they ultimately decided to place their own country's dharma on that same pedestal.

This endeavour is flowing even now through different streams. If we want to increase the number of Indian representatives in the king's court we will have to depend on the wishes of the king himself. But the desire to free our mind and make it move towards its own success depends entirely on our own strength. Any of us can move in any direction on the basis of our own strength and those of us will extend the idea of spiritual self-realization of the country. The joy of that realization is the only support in our journey towards development.

The terrible pride that one feels at the beginning of realizing such strength actually acts as an impediment towards self-realization. Instead of educating us, it lays greater emphasis on making us forget. It equates truth and falsehood and thus humiliates truth. It tends to forget that in the process of trying to know clearly what I do not possess, I get to know what I actually have. This knowing clearly is the only method of regaining our strength. Pride blurs the path of self-realization and leads us towards weakness and failure. The foundation of self-glorification rests on truth so we can never attain it through pride. The more our pride is lessened by hitting upon the walls of truth, the more we tend to know ourselves.

For quite some time there is an attempt in Ireland as in our own country to give independence to our willpower. There is naturally a lot of exuberance at such an effort for the first time and it sometimes cannot maintain its weight and becomes a laughing stock in a strange sort of way. That it had also happened in Ireland can be understood when we read the book *Hail and Farewell* by the famous Irish writer George Moore.

Anyhow, in the attempt to express the free spirit of Ireland through her own language, folklore and myths, and in that attempt at expression a few exceptional talents have found their own field. The poet Yeats is one of them. He has been able to conjoin the message of Ireland to world literature gloriously.

When Yeats carried into the world of literature the success of the Irish literary flag, from a few years before that, enterprise had weakened in Irish literature. Then the period of political upsurge in Ireland resulted in crude political satire. To give importance to shrewd political ideology during that time, patriotic feelings were done away with.

One critic of Yeats wrote:

> During that time the messenger of war appeared once again; this time no resounding echoes of any revolutionary-era social messages were heard along with the sparks of tremendous emotion. The all-embracing human spirit that has realized itself and whose invisible fingers are touching all the great creative mysteries in man's world, that self-satisfied human spirit covered the entire world with peace. Expressing the greater freedom of the human soul within himself Yeats once again revived the spirit of revolt with deeper and finer strength. Now it was no longer the turbulence outside; the

> poet spoke of the internal feelings of the human spirit and that was about Ireland and all human beings. He thought deeply and abandoned the 50-year-old poetic style. But the manner in which he gave completeness to the art of writing was actually an improved version of the writing style of the older poets. His poetic vision has focused on the minutest details of natural beauty and he has been able to capture the internal music of the beauty of sound in his rhythms. All those ingredients of thought which he had woven in the unparalleled verse lyrics of his initial years is a legacy of his Druid ancestors; that entered into the mysteries of the blooming manifested nature and has realized the oneness of nature, man and God.

The critic has further written:

> It was with the publication of *The Wanderings of Oisin*—in 1889, if I remember alright—that Yeats sprang into the front rank of contemporary poets, and threatened to add to the august company of the immortals. In the qualities by which he succeeded—an exquisite delicate music, intensity of imaginative conviction, intimacy with natural and (dare I say?) supernatural manifestations—he was typically Celtic.

This imaginative conviction is very true of Yeats. Imagination for him is not a mere plaything; whatever he has seen in the light of his imagination he has been able to accept in his life as truth. That means imagination is not a poetic usage only, it is the tool of his life; it is through imagination that he gets the resources for his soul. I have realized this whenever I have had an intimate conversation with him. I have not as yet got the opportunity of reading his complete poems and of realizing that he is a poet, but from the moment I have met him I have been able to realize that he is touching every sphere around him energetically through his imaginative spirit.

37, Alfred Place
South Kensington, London
Bhadra 19, 1319 B.S.
[First published in *Prabasi, Kartik* issue, 1319 B.S.]

Chapter 13

Stopford Brooke

There is perhaps nothing to be ashamed about feeling happy when someone likes any of my writings. Actually it is a matter of boasting to say that one is not happy about it. Whenever I have published a book, there lies in it an ingrained hope that people will like it. If that is considered as pride then we can say that the publication of the book itself is a matter of pride.

At some leisure moments I had attempted to translate a few of my own poems and songs into English prose. I never had the pride that I can write in English; hence I did not expect laurels for my English compositions. But the pleasure of listening to my own emotions in a foreign tongue and accepting it in a new way engulfed me. I was examining the identity of my heart in a new garb.

After I came to England, when some of these translations reached my friend, he accepted them with special warmth and grace. He got a few copies made and gave them to a few littérateurs here to be read. They have liked this writing of English in a foreign hand. One of the probable reasons for this could be that the power of my English compositions is not strong enough to annihilate the foreign essence from them completely.

A copy of these translations had reached Stopford Brooke. One day he invited me to dinner for this reason. He is old, probably past 70.There is an inflammation in the blood channel in one of his legs; he found it difficult to move and sat with that leg raised on a stool. Age forces some people into submission and with some it establishes a relationship of friendship and resides like one. Age could neither influence his body nor his mind. His youthfulness was amazing. I repeatedly kept on thinking that when you can see youthfulness in an old man, then you really see youth at its best. This was because that youthfulness was the real thing; it does not know how to decay along with the flesh and blood body; on its own strength it could keep all disease and decay at bay. He had a voluminous body; his face was handsome, only his ailing leg reminded me of the Mahabharata episode—just as Arjuna had struck an arrow at Dronacharya's feet before his fight with Dronacharya began as a mark of obeisance to his master, so also old age had hurled the first arrow of the launch of the war near this man's feet.

The life that God had blessed him with, he has made it in every which way an ingredient of happiness—he has avid passion for painting, poetry, natural beauty and the multitudinous nuances of human life in society. Age has not diminished his ability to derive pleasure from the sensory world around him. This capability of absorption is youth.

I had earlier read his religious treatise and poetic criticism. That day I saw his indulgence in painting too. A lot of paintings of natural scenery lay stacked in the corner of his room. All these were drawn from his own imagination. My painter friend praised these paintings very much. These were not done for exhibiting or entertaining other people—they were the manifestation of the feelings within his own heart. I was thinking about these things—he was quite old, had to write a lot and was not fully healthy—yet none of these could deplete his enthusiasm. The intensity of life force endowed him with the space to play amidst so much work. Really, we get to know about one's spirit from such playfulness. The wealth of man lies in the freedom that surrounds his essential work. I have noticed this in many people who have achieved fame in this country. Their lives are not stuck around their primary work or employment; there is always some empty space all around enabling them to move about freely. I have seen a great scientist do Chinese painting as his main hobby. They have a significant amount of spare and extra space in their life's storage. For many of them, business is just a part of their lives. The office is just one room in their dwelling house.

After climbing a lot of steps I met him in a small room upstairs. We had plenty of time to converse in private. From his talk I understood that though at some point of time there was the necessity for an external framework of Christianity—something that in English is called *creed*—this was now preventing the essence of pure religion to percolate among people. Whenever the mind of man grows above its shelter, then there is no greater enemy than that shelter. The main reason why many people in this country have become adverse towards religion is because of its external form. He told me, 'There is no essence of any religion or any *creed* in your poems and this, I believe, will be very helpful for the people of our country.'

At one point during the conversation he asked me whether I believed in the idea of rebirth. I told him that I do not have any specific imagination beyond my present life and also do not feel it essential to think about it. But when I think about it, then I feel that it can never be that within the stream of my existence this human life is an aberration—it was never so before, it will never be so later; the reason for which this life has expressed itself in a specific form, the same reason that helped it to begin in the first place will also completely end it in this life too. It seems possible that repeated physical birth is making the self move towards a completeness. But I cannot believe that in his earlier birth man was an animal and so in the next birth he will also have an animal body. This is because there is a systematic habit in nature and it is unlikely that its harmony will suddenly break. Stopford Brooke said that he too believed in rebirth; his belief is that after various births when we will complete a cycle of life, then the complete memory of our earlier births will become alive. I liked these words. I felt that after we finish reading a poem, then the equivalent mood occurs in our minds simultaneously; if we do not complete it then we cannot get its clue. Each of us is weaving a garland of life through a reason; for different reasons, the end of the stringing does not signify the end, but only the completion of a story. It is then that we can accept everything clearly.

One thing that I have noticed about all thoughtful and meditative people here is that they really want to do away with that which is unfair and unjust. It may seem superfluous to say that, but it is not so. It does not seem out of place here to state that the nation that rules a country far away from its own, and with those subordinate countries is entwined in various relations of self-interest, cannot live without diminishing the values of fair and unfair with regard to those other nations. As long as it is necessary for their own benefit to keep the other nation under their control, they cannot keep their feelings of righteousness about freedom of individual unblemished. The good sense that makes man respect the independence of his fellow human beings, diminishes with his enhancing desire to keep others under his own control. But, this good sense is the greatest support of man vis-à-vis national development.

Under such conditions when I see a group of intellectuals here who honour national justice more than national self-interest, then I understand that it is just like the human body—if one part of the body is open to diseases, then the other part is steadily working to maintain healthy conditions. As long as this exists, there is hope. This good-sense is present among many thoughtful individuals here.

Here the field of abstract idea and the factory for actual work exist side by side. Here the throne of political rule and the altar of religious laws exist close to each other. This is why these two combined together make the two-wheeled chariot move. Sometimes there comes a time when the smoke from work clouds and darkens all the winds of thoughts; during that period even in literature and poetry loud beats of the wrestler's bragging try to cover up all music; suddenly there arises the poison of jingoism in the blood of the people of this land and in those days of bullying, people tend to evaluate humanitarian values as expressions of the god-fearing, weak and coward. But even during that crazy aberration the sense of the fair and just does not totally disappear; that is why there was a group of people here even during the Boer War who accepted all the criticism and hatred of their entire nation and still tried to keep the flag of justice flying high. These are the same people who, having been condemned by their own people, and being called enemies of the country, have endured and still attempt to save her from her sinful deeds.

But the British rule prevalent in India is located largely in the working arena. There are no significant winds of imagination to rectify the poison of work there. This is why this poison is gradually accumulating inside the country. The Englishman who in his young age graduates in a difficult examination and then goes over to rule the country, lands himself right inside that poisonous and heated atmosphere. The intoxication of power and the adulation of servitude get ingrained in his body and this sense of pride and prestige does not want to bend down even before religion. It is strange that those British thoughtful intellectuals who constantly recite the mantras to control perversion are missing there. This is why the British in India cannot come close to the heart of the Indian people; this is why the British in India cannot get the bigger perception of India. We are very petty in their eyes; our literature, our religious movements, our nationalistic fervour are all unknown to them. We are shoppers in their market, clerks in their offices, the babus of their barristers and the convict and complainant in their courts. They do not look at us with a complete humanitarian outlook; hence they do not get a complete picture of our human identity. Under such conditions the arrangement for maintenance of proper administration can be concrete but greater things are lost in the process. If we are unable to get the man along with the good thing that he imparts, then we are unable to accept the gift wholeheartedly because order and administration is not welfare. Hence that gift neither benefits the bestower, nor satisfies the receiver.

[First published in *Prabasi, Kartik* issue 1319 B.S.]

Chapter 14

The Thoughtful Society of England

I felt that I have moved away from the external crowds and entered the crowd within the heart. The more I came into contact with the writers and thoughtful people in this country, the more I felt that they have too many emotions in the pattern of their thoughts.

From the way people are always running around and the motor vehicles rushing, it is evident that their society is attracting everyone's energy with full force. No one has any time; work has to be completed quickly, and this society will not let anyone lag behind. Lagging behind implies being defeated. Whenever I see this tremendous rush to move forward, I try to imagine who is sitting in front of them. He beckons but does not show himself. He raises his hands day and night like waves upon waves far away in the wide expanse of the blue ocean, but from some cave at the top of the mountain the waterfalls are violently rushing down at a rapid pace by pushing aside the pebbles on both sides without asking anyone about their destination.

Just as in the field of exterior work there is much shouting and running around, so also in the field of thoughts. There is no limit to the number of people who are also rushing with their thoughts. Their inner feelings are always flowing out in the daily newspapers, weekly papers, monthly and quarterly magazines, in educational institutions, in the parliament and in books and pamphlets. Of whatever kind and quality they might be, the mental strength of each person is continuously being drained. Only one call emanates from the heart of this country and that is heard everywhere—'We want more'. The call is very loud and pulling, hence no one has the patience to wait, they get perturbed to keep quiet even for a little while. In this country the person who has supplied any thoughts to the mental storehouse of the nation gets no respite. He is expected to deliver even more and everyone will start questioning him if he doesn't. This is somewhat like the yearly cuts made on the trunk of the date-palm tree. If the sap that oozes out is comparatively less in a certain year then everyone becomes anxious.

If I could physically see the mental state of this country then I would see rush everywhere. There is so much of crowd all around that it becomes difficult to walk on the main streets and lanes, in the office areas and common places. There also some walk, some drive motorcars, some work as daily labourers and others as businessmen. But everyone is extremely busy. There is no end to this movement from early morning till midnight.

This is nothing new. We can imagine the tremendous chaos and rush in the thought pattern of this country even back in our own country with our eyes half closed in a lazy, quiet and sleepy afternoon. But when that crowd creates a pressure on your own mind then I can clearly realize its force. It doesn't take too long to realize that force when we come to the people of this country who deal with matters of the heart.

My acquaintance with these people is neither very old, nor very intimate; it is a matter of a few seconds. But even in that brief period I have been repeatedly surprised to notice one thing and that is their mental agility. The mind is always alert and ready to ignite like an electric wire; the light glows instantly at the press of a button. We need wicks, oil and flint stones to light up the oil lamps that we use. Since there is no hurry we are not worried if we are a bit late. So as per our habits the swiftness of the electric lamp is totally new.

I had read one or two novels and a book about the American civilization written by the famous contemporary writer Mr. Wells. From that I was aware that his thoughts are as sharp and as dazzling as a steel sword. The day my friend invited me to have dinner along with this writer, I felt a bit scared. I felt that a razor-sharp intelligence probably got a lot of work done in this world but such a company would probably not be that comfortable.

Anyhow I met him that evening and had a long discussion with him. At the very beginning I felt assured when I saw that the man was not like a porcupine. He was totally smooth. I also saw that his sharpness was in his thoughts and not in his nature. In reality, he had a natural compassion for human beings, a revulsion against injustice and was keen for the all-round development of man. All these attributes protect the mind from excessive thoughts and make one happy. This is something great in this country; man is always alert and there is no end to his inquisitive nature. This interest in man always keeps him alert. This is because only seeds and soil do not help in the growth of good crops; there should always be nutrients in the soil too. Man's attachment or pull towards another man is that eternal nutrient that helps all kinds of grains to grow exuberantly within his heart. I have seen many powerful men in our country but since they do not have that deep, strong and ever-present mental bonding with other men, they cannot fulfil their abilities to the fullest extent. Since men do not seek those treasures from them wholeheartedly, they are unable to draw out the complete wealth from within themselves. In a place where there is hardly any human habitation man does not grow anything for sustenance except the barest essentials and quite a lot of that is wasted. We also live in a similarly remote place where man does not filter us enough to attract our mind and heart. That is we can think a lot, but those thoughts cannot overcome the laziness and express themselves. Many people have hearts but they do not function beyond the boundaries of their own children or nephews.

Whatever it may be, after speaking to Wells I understood that the basis of all their thoughts and creative powers was man. That is why like a hunter whose only desire is to hunt, theirs was not simply a game of power. The sharpness of their thoughts was not like that of a knife but was an attribute alive with the sharpness of vision that contained within it a life and a heart.

I have also mentioned earlier that I was repeatedly surprised by another thing and that is their sharpness of thought. As long as my friend spoke to Wells, their conversation radiated with sparks of thought. Word struck word and the sparks came out on their own, without a minute's delay. So it can be clearly understood that their minds are always prepared. It is not that they deliberately go on thinking; it is the pressure from all sides that makes them think all the time. That is why they can think even while running and can also speak while thinking. The mind of the country lies behind their personal thoughts and the waves of those thoughts and uproar of words hit each other in different forms and directions. This makes the mind remain alert and expressive.

My friend is a painter, he doesn't deal with words. I have spoken to him several times and on many occasions and have noticed that whatever topic is placed before him he can instantly think seriously and speak about it with authority. This of course is not physical force but the power of thought. His perceptive feelings are also swift and strong. It does not take long for him to like something that is loveable; he doesn't have to depend on the opinion of others, and whatever he accepts he does it wholeheartedly. Since he has this capacity of accepting other people and their strength, he is able to make friends with different classes of powerful people in the country. Some of them are poets, some critics, some scientists and philosophers. Also some of them are talented, some knowledgeable, some jovial, some humorous. All of them are not destined to meet together at one place without any barriers but in his case everyone has been able to come together.

After speaking to my friend I realized that there are many subjects on which they do not have to think from the beginning because they have already done so beforehand. The trouble lies in the first phase of the thought because that is when hesitation has to be overcome; but if he has already proceeded to some extent then it becomes easier for him to move. In this country thoughts are always on the move; with the wheels moving on their own, most of the thoughts are already in the middle of the road. This is why when you speak to an educated man you instantly get a well thought-out reply and that flow of thought is very fast.

One can easily assume how happy one feels there where the pace of thought is like this. This happiness is the main component of the social interactions of the educated civil society here. The heart creates an ambience of its own for its movement within the social interactions taking place. The development of thought is not only related to delivering lectures or writing books, but to the interaction between one human being and another. While listening to their conversation I very often feel that they should be noted down and not be allowed to get scattered. A miserly human mind does not yield much good results. Where there is no capability of disseminating things there is also no means of utilizing them. If you want to keep a detailed record of each individual seed to be planted in the soil then you cannot get a big harvest. You have to scatter the seeds generously on all sides and even though some of them might be wasted, the crop in general would be worthwhile. That is why in the realm of thoughts there should be that sort of happiness which will let it grow much more than it is required. In our country among the different forms of poverty, the lack of happiness and spontaneity of the heart are the most significant.

Having been invited, I resided for a couple of days in the house of a Cambridge professor. His name was Lowes Dickinson and he was the author of *Letters from John Chinaman*. There was a great wave of oriental pride sweeping our country when that book was first published. Just as the heart of Europe is gathered around the thread of one civilization, so also we imagined and felt excited that one day the whole of Asia would rise up like a hundred-petalled lotus on the stalk of one civilization, as an offering on the feet of God. During that period I wrote a long article based on *Letters from John Chinaman* and read it at a meeting. At that time I seriously thought that the book was written by a Chinese man. Then I saw the writer. He was not a Chinaman but a thoughtful person and so belonged to every country. For the two days I was in that professor's house I spoke to him almost regularly. Just as a stream easily meets another stream, so also in a similar manner, my mind followed the exuberance of joy in his heart. There was nothing special to gain from this or make a profit. It did not help me to read any special book or listen to any particular college lecture.

It was simply the joy of the heart. As spring is not about fruits and flowers only but the southerly breeze whose warmth and wave among the flowers aids them to bloom in their complete happiness, so also here there is the spring breeze of interaction blowing around all activities aimed at development of the mind which is spreading the smell and scattering the seeds by which along with activities of life, the festivities of the soul have overwhelmed the sky. I too got a similar feeling from the house surrounded by books that this sympathetic and thoughtful professor possessed. One day when the famous mathematics professor Russell came and met him, their discussions gradually enthused my mind and made me feel happy. Mathematics dries up some minds while it enlightens others. Mr. Russell's mind seemed to be shining like a bright light. What I liked best was how that luminous thought also blended with unending beams of laughter. After dinner we would go and sit in the college garden. One day there amid the silence of the ancient trees, I listened to the conversation of these two professor friends till eleven at night. The topics of those discussions were wide ranging and included literature, sociology and philosophy. For me the memory of that night was very pleasant. On the one hand there was the eternal solitude of the natural world and in the middle of it the restless mind of man was spreading its own reverberations around and venturing to fold the world within his arms. As if high mountain peaks standing in their still gravity piercing the sky and close to their feet the gush of springs whom no one could stop; their powerful movement and their gurgling sound was constantly questioning and the deep mountains were filled with the sound and echo of the same. While sitting in that old garden of that ancient college I could feel the blending of nature and mind. The solitude of the larger world continuously expressed itself to men through speech and the world realized itself through this flow of speech, found its endless pleasure. This is what I realized that day deeply. I went on feeling that the spirit of darkness in this world is gigantic. That great darkness is expressing itself in the eternal sky through the play of lights. The path of that light is always moving and quivering—it expresses itself somewhere as flames, somewhere in sparks, somewhere for a split second and somewhere brightly for a long duration—but this moving light actually conveys the message of that great darkness. The constant flow of a man's heart is therefore moving through a part of the world, meandering through different paths, getting split into different branches, but nonetheless expressing the world in its own way. Wherever that expression is filled with light and is broad in its scope therein lies the justification of the existence of the world in its festivity of happiness and wealth. In that silent night the soft voices of the two friends conversing with each other made me feel the happiness and wealth of the world within the heart of man.

[First published in *Tattwabodhini Patrika*,
Kartik issue, 1319 B.S.]

Chapter 15

The English Village and the Clergy

It is not always the case that a man is able to judge which profession will suit him the best. This is why the wheels of the chariot of work groan so much as it moves along in the world. The man who should have opened a grocery store becomes a school teacher, the man who was born to be a police inspector has to work as a priest. Such discrepancies do not create much of a problem in other businesses but they certainly do so in the business of religion. This is because if a man cannot stick to the truth as far as religion is concerned, then not only does he invite failure, but he also creates misfortune.

There is a great discrepancy between the ideals of Christianity and the nature of the people of this country—the norms of total humility and charity laid down in the Christian scriptures do not seem to go with the people here. Right from ancient times, the urge to fight with nature and other human beings and the excitement of winning battles has been flowing in their veins through successive generations. This is why when those who should have been enrolled in the army are appointed as clergy, the colour of religion, instead of being white turns crimson. This is also why we do not find the clergy in Europe always on the side of peace or totally committed to the welfare and justice of all mankind. During times of war they especially make god their commander and make the worship of god a preface for bloodshed.

It is often seen that clergyman are unable to deal justly with those people whom they consider to be heathens. They feel as if these people have been created by some other god who is opposed to the Christian god. Hence they give the impression that by humiliating these people they will increase the glory of their own god. This hostility, this naked rivalry, has been always used by the clergy to torture people from other religions. Just like soldiers with weapons, they have tried to triumph by hurting other people.

This is the reason why we Indians have such a negative feeling about the clergy. We have always felt that they are totally different from us. They are ready to convert us into Christians but not prepared to be one with us. They will conquer us but will not ever treat us as their equals. They should have taken on the responsibility of uniting one nation with another. It should have been their duty to build bridges between men so that one race could maintain good relations with another and also do justice to one another. But the opposite has proved to be true. The Christian clergy have depicted a distorted picture of non-Christians and have portrayed their religion, society and customs in the worst possible light to their own countrymen. Surely every nation can be treated in such a way that either its meanness or greatness is made to stand out. But certainly every nation should be judged by its superior qualities. Vanity and the lack of love in the hearts of these people are the chief obstacles preventing them from exercising true judgment. It can be expected from the people who have given themselves to the love of god that they would overcome such impediments. By demeaning other races, and creating a big divide between Christians and non-Christians, these clergymen have created a great gulf of suspicion between people, to an extent hitherto unimaginable. They have put on communal dark glasses to view other people in their bid to spread their religion. There is always a big difference between the ruler and the ruled and this is the pride that comes from being powerful. This acts as a big impediment preventing human interaction. The clergy have made this pride even larger than religion and societal laws. Thus even Christianity has become a handicap for our union; in fact, it has kept us from displaying the best in us.

However, I have found proof that we cannot generalize about any sect. I have met a Christian clergyman after coming here who is less of a clergyman and more of a Christian—someone in whom religion has not asserted itself aggressively as a business proposition but has blended and revealed itself through his whole life. He is a person about whom no one will think, 'He doesn't belong to us, but to another group.' He has made me believe wholeheartedly that he is a person who is happy to see truth and well-being prevail in all men and does not feel envious because it is not an exclusively Christian attribute. What is even more surprising is that his workplace is India. There is a great obstacle for any Christian in India wanting to remain a true Christian since he is the king there. Politics there is the spouse of religion. Often, it is the Queen Bee. This is why the clergy in India have not been able to empathize with Indian life. There is an intense conflict between their national interests and ours and at one point they are not able to listen to their guru and lower their heads. He had asked his followers to conquer the world with humility, but that apparently is a law meant for heaven. These people are the gods of this world.

The person whom I am speaking of is Reverend Andrews. The people of India know him well. He has earned the heaven-sanctioned right to be one with us by completely suppressing the regal attitude that his Englishness had given him. I consider myself privileged to have been a witness to the way in which the loveliness and liberal ideas of Christianity have become so clearly a part of his life.

One day he said to me, 'Before going back to your country you should go and see the households here. A lot of transformation has taken place in the cities so you will not get the true picture of domestic life unless you go to the villages.' Mr. Andrews arranged for my stay for a few days with one of his friends who worked as a priest in a village in Staffordshire.

The month of August in this country is considered to be part of the summer season. During this time the people from the city become impatient to breathe country air. In our country we interact freely with nature because the sky and the sunlight are so easily available to us. We do not have to make any special arrangement to come into contact with them. But here people are always eager to unveil the beauty of nature and their desire to possess it is never satiated. On every holiday they form groups and rush to wherever there are open fields—leaving the city on long vacations. This is how nature always keeps them on the move and does not allow them to settle down anywhere. The holiday trains are full of people and seats are impossible to find. Blending with the flock of city-bred people, I too left for the countryside.

Our host was waiting for us at the station with an unhooded car. The sky was overcast when we boarded the car. The village revealed itself to us that canopied morning amid the pale covering of the sky. En route, it started to rain.

When we reached the house, his wife took us to the sitting room where the fireplace had been lit. It was not an old parish home but had been newly built. There were no ancient trees in the adjacent garden narrating the chronicles of forgotten human memories through their murmuring leaves. The garden was new, and had been probably created by the present owners. The multi-coloured flowers blooming by the dark green grass, had opened for feast the unrestrained doors of unlimited beauty for the hungry eyes. I had never seen so much liveliness and such abundance of trees and flowers as during the English summer. It is really difficult to convey in words the density and the beauty of the dark green colour of the grass here; one has to see it to believe it.

The rooms in the house were neat and tidy; the library full of readable books; there were no signs of neglect both inside and outside. This aspect of all civilized English houses strikes me as distinctive. Compared to us they use many more things for comfort and decoration of their houses but the owners take good care of even the smallest thing in each room. They understand quite well that being slack in one's affairs actually means demeaning oneself. This consciousness affects all their work, whether big or small. They do not demean the dignity of man and hence they make their houses of use in all respects; attempting to make their own surroundings, their society and their country fine in all respects. They are not willing to pardon lapses anywhere and for whatever reason.

Our host Mr. Outram took me out for a walk in the late afternoon. By then the rain had stopped but there was no dearth of clouds in the sky. Just as the men here always move around in black hats and grey clothes, the gods here seem to don very sombre and formal clothing. But the beauty of the countryside was not covered up by these sombre overcast shadows. My eyes were filled with the soothing sight of deep green undulating fields divided by fences made of creepers. Though hilly, the place was devoid of sharp folds. The passionate outbursts of the soil sloped down and met one another just as the melodious tunes of a raga in our country meld harmoniously into one another at the pull of the note. It seemed as if some god was silently playing the lyre of the earth in raga Meghamallar. The glorious pride of the lofty mountains in the hilly states of our country was not on view here. Looking around on all sides, it seemed as if one could see wild nature completely tamed here; just as instructed by the dictates of Shiva's disciple Nandi, his favourite bull bowed down its horns and silently laid his soft and smooth body at the feet of his master, scared to raise his voice and disturb his meditation.

On the way Mr. Outram discussed something important with a man he had met on the way. The topic they were discussing was the following: to encourage farmers to build gardens around their houses, a committee had been formed to judge the best garden and award a prize for the same. The competition had ended a few days ago and this man had won the prize. Mr. Outram took me to see a few homesteads of the farmers of the village. Everywhere the farmer had taken great pains to grow flowers and vegetables all around his house. These people work in their gardens in the evening, having laboured the whole day in the fields. In the process, they become so attached to these trees and plants that they do not mind putting in the extra labour. Another good effect of this craze for gardening is that it keeps the addiction to drinking at bay. The attempt to enhance external beauty gradually develops internal peace in one. I have seen how Mr. Outram is also involved in other developmental activities of these villagers and have realized how wonderful such a life devoted to the welfare of others could be. The succour of the nectar that is there in the service to God has made him as mellow as a sweet ripe fruit. His house is lit by the lamp of piety; studies and meditation clean it everyday. I will never be able to forget how simple and beautiful his hospitality was.

I could now clearly see how each of these clergymen had become the pivotal point of a cluster of these villages. This countrywide arrayed effort has awakened a spirit of growth and development in the remote villages. Thus religion is spread as welfare all over this country. By such immense initiatives all places of habitation in this country are strung together in the manner of a necklace. Only those of us who are at a loss unable to avail the fruits of such collective endeavour can know how beneficial such initiatives can be.

Man cannot build a system so perfect that it can ward off spuriousness or corruption permanently. Everyone in this country is aware that in an age of enlightenment some gaps have opened up between religious theory and practice. I have heard from several good people here that they find it impossible to go to church. They do not want to commit the sin of trying to believe in things that they cannot accept without questioning. In this way they have totally abandoned their faith in a religion that has become worn out in various ways. It is during such times that some wily old men have taken refuge within the folds of religion to corrupt it even more. Nowadays there are surely many clergymen who preach things that they themselves do not believe in; these men fool even themselves by attempting to believe what they preach. There is no doubt that such forms of corruption are harming society in different ways. Always, holding on to the form of religion blocks its main door in such a manner that only small and petty things are able to enter within and great things are left lying outside. This is the reason why all intellectually agile and humane men of Europe have fallen outside the purview of European religious rule. Such a situation can in no way ever serve humanity.

But Europe's life energy is protecting her soul. It does not get stuck anywhere. Movement is in its nature and so it is hitting against all obstacles on its way and denuding them. The manner in which Christianity has constrained itself and is causing an impediment to the flow of things needs to be altered by being hit back and widened in turn. This process is going on daily; what the great thinkers define as true Christianity is something that has at last done away with its crude external covering. This Christianity does not believe in the Trinity, does not accept Jesus as a prophet or believe in the unnatural miracles described in the holy book of Christianity and it cannot be regarded as a middlepath also. In Europe at present there is a great upheaval in matters religious. It is certain that it will never allow its traditional religious beliefs to lag behind its total developmental plans or burden itself permanently with such a huge load.

In any case, the way the clergy have bound up the entire nation within the net of religious ideals, despite sometimes creating impediments to prevent the development of the country, have no doubt also managed to vibrate the finer strings of the country in the most effective way. The Brahmins in our country also had this sort of work as their goal but because their work was tied to their caste consciousness, they inevitably lost sight of their responsibilities. The higher the goal a particular Brahmin sets for himself the more he will have to rely on unique capabilities and special skills of a person. But whenever this responsibility is thrust on a particular class for generations, such idealism gets curbed considerably. A man can be a Brahmin only if he is born in a Brahmin household—this simple and unnatural falsehood has been followed blindly in our society and hence the religion has turned moribund and is beset by superstitions. The Brahmin whom society has been forced to respect is a person who does not consider it necessary that he should earn respect for himself by his deeds. What he does try is to rule society with the whip of his sacred thread but in doing so he keeps debasing it although, because of the blindness induced by custom, we do not manage to understand that this is what is happening. I do not believe that all the clergymen here have accepted the ideals of true Christianity and practice it perfectly in their lives devotedly; but because they are not clergyman by birth, they are answerable to society and therefore cannot afford to stain their character. Thus, at the very least they try to display to the nation a purity of character and their devotion to their faith. Whatever our own scriptures might say, our people do not feel ashamed to undergo religious ceremonies done by impious Brahmins. This leads to a big gap between our religious beliefs and our piety; consequently our humanity keeps getting debased everyday. Here in England however, society will never forgive an immoral clergyman; he may not be very religious but he has to be seen as morally upright. It is through this means that society here is able to affirm its humanity and needless to say, it is thus that it has been able to develop its human resources.

That is why I was saying that the clergy here has managed to come up with a system of religious morality for the whole country that depends on plain living and plain thinking. But this is not sufficient in many cases. Again and again, when this country faces religious problems, the clergy do not try and solve them through Christ's message. Here I find them deviating from their responsibility they have undertaken of establishing Christ in the heart of their countrymen. How did all the clergy of this country view the Boer War when it broke out? Why are the clergymen quiet, now that two fat European ladies are attempting to divide Persia into two halves? Much injustice is done in India in relation to the recruitment of coolies, the system of employing them, in the administrative system there and in the manner in which the English misbehave with the natives. Is it not the case that there are many instances of abuse which necessitate these people to follow Christ and stand next to weak and humiliated people? Have we ever witnessed such heavenly sights? There is a saying in English, 'Penny wise, pound foolish'. In matters of religion we see the same thing everyday in all big Christian nations—they want to be secure in their personal moral values, but elsewhere the entire nation gets into a battle line and shamelessly commits major sinful acts resulting in a lot of intolerable suffering in terms of space and time. I have seen many noble-hearted people of this country stand up against this collective weakness, but how many clergymen are there among them? In fact, if we conduct a survey amongst them, it will be revealed that most of them do not have faith in the way Christianity is practised. On the other hand, if there is the slightest deviation from the traditional rites practised in the Church, the entire clergy create a ruckus. Was this the reason why Jesus shed his blood? What positive message do the clergy of all these Christian nations spread when they keep holding on to the little money in their religious funds while remaining oblivious of big shareholdings of the company going down the drain? I can see everyday that they value their god as they would a farthing but can also humiliate him for the sake of a sovereign. There are a few gentlemen among the clergy who are true friends of the world, but that is due to their own magnanimity. But if you look at them as a whole and entrust them with your religion then you are sure to be trodden to some extent. This creates a kind of caste system and though it is in many ways much better than the hereditary caste system, it also retains some of the poisons of the system. Because religion can free man it should be kept completely open. But if religion is confined within the barriers created by a group, then gradually its meaner side becomes more well-known than its prominent side; external elements begin to enshroud internal ones, and temporal issues keep plaguing it on a daily basis. This is why, in spite of the country being full of clergymen, political leaders do not hesitate to resort to loot and murder. The clergy do not have that sacred halo which would allow them to get rid of the scar of evil from spreading publicly and taking a monstrous shape.

[First published in *Tattwabodhini Patrika*,
Pous issue, 1319 B.S.]

Chapter 16

Music

We have reached this country at the end of summer and now the music sessions here are coming to a close. Now there are no concerts or musical performances by any great artist. After crossing several oceans the birds come to the arbour here in summer and after that they break off the gathering and go back. Human music also does not play here at all seasons. It has a special time and during that period different expert musicians come here from different places and worship Saraswati, the goddess of music.

Once upon a time we too had such musical sessions in our country. Musicians from all over the country would come and gather at the houses of rich patrons during religious festivals. In those music festivals the entrance of ordinary people was free and open to all. Then Lakshmi, the goddess of wealth and Saraswati, the goddess of learning would meet together and the music of spring would blow over the hearts of all people in the country. In every country once upon a time, the traditionally aristocratic people protected the arts, literature and music of that country. In Europe the ordinary people have now occupied the place of that aristocracy;

the way the people in our country get together to perform a public function that kind of a culture has spread all over Europe. This collective enterprise sponsors musicians to listen to their music; it is through their munificence that the poverty of the poor poet is done away with and the painter draws pictures to get the blessings of Lakshmi. In our country at present the rich people have no responsibility of their wealth; what they do with it is only to increase the profits of Lazarus Oslar, Hamilton Herman and Mackintosh Burn companies. The ordinary people have neither the power nor the taste for it. In our country even Lakshmi has disowned the Kalabodhu, the wife of Ganesha, and she does not even have shelter in Ganesha's abode.

It is fortunate that this time within a few weeks after coming to London there was a Handel festival organized in the auditorium of the Crystal Palace. The famous music composer Handel was German but he spent most of his life in England. He had composed music to certain sections of the Bible and those have received a lot of favour in this country. During the Handel festival, these songs are sung by hundreds of singers to the accompaniment of hundreds of musical instruments. This year's festival was performed by 4,000 singers and musicians.

I was present in this festival. Singers and musicians sat on every step of the gallery of this huge auditorium. It was so huge that one could not see anybody without the help of binoculars, as if clusters of human clouds had gathered there. The men and women singers sat in different sections according to the differing pitch—base, alto and soprano—of their voices. They wore clothes of the same colour and design and it seemed as if someone had woven lines and lines of silk on a huge canvas.

The music arose from 4,000 voices and instruments. Among them, even one person did not go out of tune. Strains of 4,000 tunes danced along and came out together, without hurting each other. Though not the same tune but a huge accumulation of different tunes. This huge strength that existed in combining the different tunes in a harmony of flawless completeness surprised me. There was no strain of laziness or casualness both within and without this awakened power. Everything beginning from their sitting position, their dress, right up to the neatness of musical art—everywhere its infallible law was combining each part to the whole.

Sometimes I opened the printed programme and tried to synchronize the words of the song with its tune. But I cannot say for sure that I found a similarity. There is no doubt that such a huge affair would be a mechanical thing . The outward shape was huge, multifarious and pure but the inner significance was suppressed. I felt as if a huge regiment of soldiers was marching along. This music had power but no enchantment.

But it would not be speaking the truth if we say that all European music was like this. This means it is not believable if we say that in all European music the perfection of form is the most important, not the emotional content of it. This is because it is clearly seen how the emotion in music has kept Europe enlivened. The attraction of the bee towards the flower is ample proof that there is honey in it; that honey might not be visible to me.

It is true that there is one big difference between the music of Europe and that of our country. The main component of European music is harmony or melodiousness of tunes while the main component of our music is ragas. Europe has kept its eyes on variety and we on unity. In world music we find different tunes emerging in different strains; one is not the echo of the other. Everyone has its own significance, and yet at the same time everything comes together to fill up the sky. Harmony is showing the huge dance of the many faces of the world through melody. But surely within it is running the song of a particular raga also, and around the melody and rhythms of that song the dance is making its unique movement successful. The music of our country is trying to capture that interim song. That solemn, secret one—found in meditation, lying still in the sky. It is the European nature to keep pace with that which is forever moving; and it is our nature to lay our ears and our hearts towards the eternal silence, to concentrate on that and pacify ourselves.

Don't we experience this in the music of our country? We can see in European music it has a connection with the play of waves and the rhythms of man. It has a direct contact with human sorrow and joy. Our music does not emerge from within the experience of man, it flows in from the outside. In European music man has lighted up his own house, the light of festivities and different colours of chandeliers. In our music, the moon has sheds its light from across the horizon. That is why I repeatedly feel that our music goes beyond our sorrow and joy. On our wedding nights, there is raga Sahana playing from a podium. But where is merriment in the tune of that raga? There is no youthful exuberance in it; it is solemn. There is pity as one musical note rolls into another within its musical folds. In our country foreign bands performing along with the music of the sehnai is a part of modern weddings that exposes the barbarity of the rich people. The difference between the two is very clear. With the tune of the foreign band is throbbing the festivity of human enjoyment and the earth is reverberating with its sound—the crowd of people laughing, merrymaking, flowers, decoration and lights everywhere is matching the exuberance in the tune of the band. But the still and dark night that encircles the merriment of the wedding, where the permanent festivities of the world beyond is bright in the silent and placid light of the stars and planets, the tune of the Sahana raga carries in the message of that place. Our music gradually opens the main gate of entertainment and brings in the Infinity among the people. Our music is a solo song, a song sung alone but it is not the song of the one that is in the corner, it is that of the one that is universal.

If the harmony is too intense then it shadows the song and wherever the song wants to remain independent, then it does not let harmony approach it. This division between the two is good for a certain period of time. Each one should be given the ease of independence to get its matured form. But that does not mean that they will remain bachelors forever. Till such time as the bride and the groom do not grow mature, they should be allowed to grow up separately. But even after that if they cannot get united then they remain incomplete. It is beyond doubt that the day of uniting song and harmony has arrived. The arrangements for such a union has also begun.

In the villages there is a market on one particular day of the week and there is one particular day in the year when a fair takes place. On that day men exchange goods with one another and fulfil the needs that each of them have. In human history too, a market day occurs in each era; on that day everyone carries their own wares in a basket and goes to collect the things other people bring along. On that day man understands that his poverty cannot be alleviated only with the things he produces; he understands that the only success of his own wealth is that it gives him the right to get things from others. This age is known in European history as the Renaissance age. The big market that the renaissance is offering at the present time has never taken place before. The main reason for this is that earlier there weren't so many approachable roads as we have at present.

Some time back a great man told me that in Europe the time for the Indian Renaissance is approaching. Europe has suddenly taken cognizance of the great historical wealth that India has in store and Europe feels that those are required by her. All this while Indian painting and architecture was looked down upon by Europe, now Europe has seen a certain glamour in it.

Very recently Europe has also started taking notice of Indian music. While in India I have seen European listeners listening in rapt attention to the raga Bageshree being played on the surbahar. One day I saw an English listener sitting in a meeting and listening to two Bengali youth singing songs from the *Sama Veda*. Both the singers put the Vedic chants in the ragas Iman Kalyan and Bhairavi and recited them as Sama songs. I had to tell him that this could not be accepted as Sama songs. I realized that making him aware was really superfluous on my part because he knew a lot more than me. He asked me to recite Vedic chants and I recited the little bit I knew. He then said, 'This is the manner in which you recite chants from the *Yajur Veda*.' I had actually recited hymns from the *Yajur Veda*. He had researched thoroughly on Vedic chants to ragas and rhythms of *dhrupad* and kheyal and it was not easy to hoodwink him. He is writing a book on Indian music.

The Modern Review often publishes articles by Mrs. Maud McCarthy. She has an exceptional talent in music from childhood. At the age of nine she had charmed her audience by playing the violin in an open concert. Unfortunately she suffered from nervous ailments in her hands and had to stop playing music. She stayed in India for some time and especially discussed South Indian music. Now she is too busy writing a book on it.

One day Dr. Coomaraswamy invited me to listen to the songs of Ratandevi. I did not know who Ratandevi was and thought that she would be some Indian lady. But I saw that she was an English lady and was the mistress of the house where we were invited.

She sat on the floor and started singing with a stringed musical instrument on her lap. I was totally surprised. This was no child's play like singing '*hilimili pania*'. She regularly followed the rules and sang Canara Malkoush and Behag ragas with appropriate *alaap*. She added the most difficult intonations and musical strains to it, started to keep the beat with her hands and did not apply English mannerism to wipe off 75 per cent of the Indianness from the singing. The only difference with our ustads was it was as if that there was no impediment in her voice, neither was there any laboured attempt in the gestures of her body or in her voice. So the form of the song began to appear untiringly and unimpeded by anything.

Those people in this country who are engaged in the discussion of Indian music are not merely doing it out of sheer curiosity; they have discovered a wonderful beauty within it. They want to savour it to the fullest extent. In fact they are eager to probably include it in their own music. Till now their number is no doubt very much limited but if even one corner catches fire then it gradually spreads out by its own force.

Here I have met Dr. Yorktrotter who is the principal of London Academy of Music. He has got some taste in Indian music. He repeatedly expressed his desire so that there could be a way through which Indian music could be discussed in London. He felt that if any rich Indian king could sponsor a veteran artist who played the *veena* and could stay in London for some time, then it would be really beneficial.

This would actually help us. Because we have lost our respect for our music and art. Its contact with our lives is becoming increasingly faint. When there is an ebb tide in the river then only the mud keeps coming out. In our world of music we have crossed over the high tide and so we are now weltering in the mud at the bottom of the river. It does the opposite task of taking a bath. The kind of music that plays over the gramophone in all our homes, the kind of songs we learn from the theatre, make it evident that the ugliness in the poverty of our hearts gets exposed and we are in fact accepting that ugliness as part of our lives. No one can free the world of cheap and spurious things at one go. There is always a group of people in all societies whose companionship cannot rise higher than that; but when that sort of people fill up the whole country, the Goddess Saraswati becomes a cheap mechanical toy. It is then that our perseverance and success become weak. So now our country will be filled up with the weeds of the gramophone and the concert parties; the golden crop that needs to be implanted is gradually dying a slow death.

One day Dr. Coomaraswamy told me, 'Maybe there will come a time when you will have to go to Europe with your music.' There are many things in our country which we are waiting to receive from Europe. Once our music crosses the ocean and once we get it back, maybe we will get it in a proper way. We have spent a long time sitting in the corner of our house and so we do not know the market value of anything. We do not have the strength to test our own things before accepting them or to understand clearly where our glory lies.

Where man's efforts stemming from an abundant life force is continuously being disseminated in different forms, where all the wealth of man is being utilized in the great enterprise of life and profits are increasing, there if we don't bring our wares, if we don't join the existing business, then we cannot know ourselves. Hence a lot of our energy is only going to be wasted. The only fear chasing us is in case we tend to forget ourselves after coming into contact with Europe. But this is not true; the opposite is true. Coming into contact with this great living force for the first time we are overwhelmed for a while but we end up enlivening our own nature. The lively literature of Europe has aroused our attempt at literary endeavours; the stronger it becomes, the more it encourages us not to imitate but leads us towards self-expression. The recent revival that we see in our art has also the European life force behind it. I believe we need that outside contact even in the field of music. We have to take it out of the old-fashioned iron safe and encash it in the outside world. We can learn to use our own music in the true and proper way only if we get well-acquainted with European music. It is sad to say that music is not part of the education of our learned people; there is no place for art and music in our factories for clerkship that we call college and it is strange that those institutions which we have established with the name of 'national', there has been laid no place also for the arts. While learning the notes by heart and collecting our degrees we have even forgotten to feel how important this is in the overall social life of man. That is why music is still within the closet of those uneducated people who do not have the open expanse of the world in front of them; as do incompetent women who have converted all their treasures into jewellery and can only carry them along but cannot utilize them fully; so much so that if even the prospect of their usage is indicated they get terrified—they feel that it is a ploy for them to lose everything.

Hence, when we could not use our wealth in a proper way, then those who can would use it for their business and find out a way to use it for the welfare of the world. We will have to wait for that particular day and only after that we can say with pride – 'No one else in the world has what we have.' The ingredients for that pride would also have to be supplied by other people.

[First published in *Bharati, Agrahayan* issue, 1319 B.S.]

Chapter 17

Social Difference

When we travel to Vilayet, then it is not simply going from one country to another; for us it is like entering a new household. The external differences of lifestyle are not that important. It is expected that there will be a difference between us and the foreigners in our dress, ornaments, eating and pleasure habits and so that doesn't bother us too much. But not only in lifestyle, there is a deeper dissimilarity in our evaluation of life and to find a sense of direction there suddenly becomes a very difficult task.

We start feeling this from the moment we board the ship. We understand that we will have to abide by the rules of another different household. This sudden change is not to the liking of man. This is why we do not try to understand it very clearly; we somehow try to follow it or feel disgusted and then utter to ourselves—their manner and behaviour is too artificial.

The truth is that what is important is the difference we have with them regarding our social position. Our society has reached and stopped at the limits of family and village. Within those limits we have evolved certain fixed rules about how to behave with one another. Keeping those limits in mind it has been decided what we should do and what we should not. Some of those rules are superficial whereas others are quite normal.

But the society with which as a target these rules have been framed is not very big in size and it is a society of relatives. So our habits are quite domesticated. You cannot smoke tobacco in front of your father, you are supposed to pay obeisance to the guru and pay him some money, the sister-in-law has to cover up her face in the presence of the elder brother-in-law and close proximity to your uncle-in-law is totally prohibited. Those rules that are outside the societal structures of this family or village are more or less based on caste(varna) differences.

It can be said that the thread of caste difference has tied our village society and families like a chain or necklace. We have reached a conclusion. India has resolved its societal problems once and for all and she feels that if this system can be permanently retained then there is nothing to worry about. That is why modern India is trying to strengthen in all manner this family and social bonding laws weaved through the convention of the four different stages in the life of a Hindu.

It has to be admitted that India had been able to find a solution to the problems it was facing at one point of time. She has somehow reconciled the differences between diverse castes, she has pacified the struggle between diverse classes; by classifying professions she has managed to contain competition and disputes and has staved off the vanity created by difference of wealth and capacity through the fence of caste difference. Though on the one hand India has maintained through all means the independence of Brahmins who are at the helm of society to the people belonging to other castes at the same time she has also spread out small and big processes through which all facilities and education could be disseminated among the others. This is why what the rich person enjoys in India is also partly distributed among the ordinary people on various pretexts and in this way by giving shelter to the ordinary and appeasing them the powerful retains his power. In our country there is no reason to go into a major clash between the rich and the poor and the necessity has not arisen by which the incapable person has to be protected by legal means.

The western society is not family oriented; it is an open and large society which is much more spread out than ours. It is more on the outside than on the inside. The concept of family that is there in our country is absent in Europe and that is why the people of Europe are spread out everywhere.

The nature of this spread-out society is such that on the one hand it is loosely assimilated and on the other it is more diverse and strong. It is like composing a prose piece. Poetry is restricted within its rhymes and that is why its binding is simpler. But the prose spreads out. That is why on the one hand it is independent and on the other its steps are bound through logic and reason, through diverse rules on ideas about the development of the mind in a greater way.

Because the English society is so spread out and because all its activities are externally motivated that is why it has to be always prepared for different social rituals. It hardly has time to wear casual domestic clothes. It has to remain dressed up because its social area is not that of relatives. Relatives pardon you, tolerate you, but you cannot expect such tolerance on the part of outsiders. Everyone has to do each and every work in due time otherwise one will encroach upon another. If the rail line belongs to me alone or is under the control of a few of my friends and relatives, then we can run the train as we wish and can even halt each other's train as and when we desire. But if we try to detain a train for five minutes in the ordinary train route where lots of trains move up and down, then there will be lots of problems and that will be difficult to tolerate. Because our society is extremely domesticated or maybe because we are habituated with domestic practices we behave with each other very loosely—we spread ourselves as much as possible, waste time and criticize formal behaviour to be a lack of fraternal feelings. This is the first thing that prevents us in English society—there one cannot act in a carefree manner and then expect that people will pardon us. They have created different rules that will on an average benefit the maximum number of people. They have set up fixed rules for meeting each other, for invitation formalities, for dressing up, for entertaining guests. If we try and impose the laxity that we display with relatives in a place that is not actually a society of relatives, then everything turns out to be horrible and life becomes impossible.

Till now this wide European society has not come up with any solutions. It has made an effort through certain rules and regulations in external rituals and behaviour to retain self-restraint and gracefulness, but is unable to make arrangements by which the internal strife with each other can be resolved. Europe is only running through experimentation, change and revolution. There is a constant rivalry cropping up between men and women, between religious society and professional society, between the power of the ruler and the ruled, between businessmen and worker groups. It has not pacified itself like the halo round the moon. Even now it is ready like a volcano waiting to erupt.

But how can we say that we have solved all our problems, have finalized our social structure and are resting as peacefully as dead bodies? Even though time has elapsed, we can retain the system for some time, but we cannot keep the situation in chains. We are facing the entire world, now we cannot do with our domesticated society; these people are not merely our fathers, grandfathers or uncles, they are outsiders, they belong to different countries and so we should be extremely alert while interacting with them. If we are absent-minded and behave in a loose manner then one day we will be totally unfit to act.

We are proud of our tradition but it is not at all true that the society of India has not evolved through history. In different situations even India had to go through newer revolutions—there is no doubt about that—and history is replete with instances. But I don't want to even utter such feelings that it is the end of all treading for her and from now on till eternity she will just be there and hold on to her traditionality. Society gets fatigued after each large revolution; during that time it shuts its doors, switches off all lights and prepares to go to sleep. After the Buddhist revolution India had gone off to sleep latching her doors and windows with the hook of strict laws. She was sleepy. But to boast about this as eternal sleep will become a laughable though pitiable thing. Sleep is good only during the night, when there are no crowds of people outside, and when all the big shops and markets are shut down. But in the morning when everyone is awake and there is activity all around, if you lie down quietly and shut down all the old doors and windows then you will be the loser.

The rules of the night are very simple. Its arrangements are sparse and its requirements are very little. That is why we can complete all our tasks and go to sleep in an unperturbed manner. Then things remain lying where they were kept because there is no one to move them. The arrangements during the day are not so simple and to complete the job once and for all in the early morning does not mean that one can relax and smoke tobacco the rest of the day. Work keeps on pouring down our necks, we have to go on attempting new things and if we cannot adjust ourselves to the flow of the outside world then everything else falls out of place.

For some time India has spent her nights in a system of

strict and fixed set of rules. That does not mean that that situation will permanently remain very comfortable. Getting a beating is most painful and difficult especially when it falls upon a sleeping body. Daytime is the period to receive such blows. That is why it is most comfortable to remain awake during the daytime.

It is time for us to wake up whether we wish it or not, whether we are full of laziness or not. We are constantly being hurt both internally and externally in society and so we are sad. We are suffering from poverty and famine. The society is breaking down; the joint family system is being split into bits and pieces. And the role of the Brahmins in society has become so demeaning that with the aid of Brahmin societies and such other things Brahmins keep on shouting out loudly in order to prove their existence and thus only attest to their weakness. The panchayat system in the village, worn in the neck by the government's chaprasi, has committed suicide and its ghost is dominating the village; the food in the country is incapable of satiating the small village schools; due to famine they are now relying on the charity of government dole; the rich people of the country have doused the light in their birthplaces and are roaming around in Kolkata in motor cars, and people of noble descent are ready to sacrifice their entire wealth and their daughters at the feet of a graduate groom. There is no point in blaming the Kaliyuga, or the foreign king or the native English-speaking people for this misfortune. The truth is that our lord of daytime has sent his chaprasi and he will not stop till such time he can drag us out of our traditional bedrooms. So we cannot forcibly close our eyes and try to create the night at odd hours. The world that has come to our threshold has to be welcomed inside our house; if we don't give it a cordial welcome then it will break open our doors and gain entry. Hasn't the door been broken yet?

So once again we have to think about resolving our problems. It cannot be done by imitating Europe but we have to learn from her. Learning and imitating are not the same thing. Actually if we learn in the correct way then we will be relieved from the art of imitating. If we cannot know the other truly then we cannot understand the truth ourselves.

But I was saying that we cannot adjust ourselves in the European society with our loose domestic habits. We can never prepare ourselves in any way. It seems that everyone is pushing us aside, no one is waiting for us for a moment. We are pampered human beings, we feel out of place without our relatives in society. After coming here I have noticed that since our students are not used to entering other people's houses, most of them come here and learn things by heart but they do not keep any contact with the society here. The society here is large and so it has more responsibilities. Only if we undertake those responsibilities can we find a sort of connection with the people of this society. If we cannot connect then we shall be deprived of the greatest learning prevalent here. This is because society is the greatest truth here. In reality the greatest strength, the greatest sublimity is in the society here and not in the battlefield. Sacrifice and self-respect suitable for a broad-minded society are being expressed at every step. They are nurtured here and are preparing themselves in different ways to sacrifice their lives for the welfare of man. In modern India, the educated class of people still consider school education to be the true education. They are deprived of the education of greater society. Even after coming here and entering the school factory, if they come out simply as mechanical things and do not enter the birthplace of humanity visible here then they will be deprived even after coming to a foreign country.

[First published in *Tattwabodhini Patrika, Ashwin* issue, 1319 B.S.]

Chapter 17

Justification of Limits

At times we hear that one cannot attain a completeness in life through poetry. If you do not move the worship of God from the world of poetics to the world of domesticity then it does not attain the firmness of truth.

I myself have thought of it occasionally when my spirits are depressed. But I also know that these thoughts are like the spread of mirage. Among all the sins that mislead man, greed is the most important. It tells man, 'There isn't truth in what you are; the truth lies outside it.'

But the Upanishads say, *Ma Gridhaha Kasyasiddhanam,* not to be greedy about the wealth of others. In other words we should not expend our desires beyond our limits.

The sloka in the Upanishads also mentions the reason for this. It states that the Supreme Being encompasses everything, hence, people who possess Him within themselves do not need anything else. When we don't realize the wealth in ourselves, then we understand that the wealth lies in someone else. But the reason that we have not found this wealth within ourselves, is the same reason we may not find it elsewhere.

Just as limitations are a fact of life, so also is limitlessness. When we try to look at both these factors separately, then we fall into a sort of trap. We make a mistake and think that if we cross our own limits then we will achieve limitlessness—as if committing suicide is the path to eternal life. It seems as if we will be pleased to become anything else except ourselves. But we tend to forget that being oneself and being someone else is the same thing. If I am a failure as myself then I shall not be relieved by becoming another myself. If there is a hole in the earthen pot and all the water inside gets drained out then it is not the fault of the water. A similar thing would happen even if you poured milk or honey in it.

There is only one thing to think about in life and that is being true. It is merely worthless thinking whether I would become a poet or a worker or anything else. The meaning of truth is that I should discern my limitations definitely. If I don't make up my mind and get enticed by wrong hopes, then I shall stray from the practice of truth.

We consider pride and greed as sin because we are unable to understand correctly our limitations. It prevents us from acquiring knowledge about our limitations and misguides us into believing that we are more than what we actually are. From this arises all sorts of sadness, jealousy and rivalry in the world. All the sorrow, conflict, wrangles are born from this rather than anything else. To try to prove by force that falsehood is basically true is the origin of all inauspiciousness.

We have a deep attraction for Infinity and that provides the impetus in our lives. It is not beneficial if we neglect that attraction and sit idle. We have to gain Infinity and that is our pleasure.

But we have to gain that Infinity within our own limitations and there is no other way out. We believe in the false notion that Infinity cannot be attained within limits. It is true that other limited things cannot fit in completely within one particular limitation. But that does not work in the case of Infinity. He is limitless even within a single grain of sand. That is why when we want to control even a grain of sand in its entirety we find that we are incapable of doing it until and unless we are able to grasp the entire world. This is because at one point it is connected with the entire universe and it has one aspect which can never be exhausted.

Our endeavour is that we will realize the expression of Infinity within our own limitations. This is because the pleasure of the Infinite has created a limitation within myself and His movement is within those limits. It is therefore wrong to assume that we will get to know Him better if we demolish His abode.

The beauty of the rose is that there is a limitlessness about it and that is because it is in its entirety a rose—there is no uncertainty or doubt about it. That is why there is something in the rose which is as clear as the sun and the moon and all other beautiful things in the world. Because it is a definite truth that it is a rose that is why its relation with the entire world is also true.

In reality indistinctness is failure, hence the expression of the Supreme Being is stalled there, His pleasure concealed. His pleasure is successful when it takes a form. The limitless is true and beautiful within limits. That is why in the history of creation, the blooming of beauty is gradually becoming more and more expressive; the tryst with the limitless is but the journey from one limitation to another. The journey of the bud to the flower, the flower to the fruit, from beauty to more manifest beauty.

That is why man desires to know himself clearly. The meaning of knowing oneself clearly is to get it within limits. The successfulness of life is attained when one can steer oneself away from the various dispersion of many roads and many false hopes and establish oneself clearly within limits.

Until and unless we learn to swim we spread our hands and feet in a haphazard way. As soon as we learn good swimming then our efforts are embraced within certain limits and then it expresses itself beautifully. A bird looks beautiful when it flies because there is no hesitation in its flight which is regulated, meaning that it has found its fixed limits. This attainment of the limits is creation, that is truth and to reach the infinite through limitations is beauty or happiness. To deviate from the limits is ugly; it is unhappy and destructive.

Poetic language with much ornamentation is a failure, when it is false, that is, when it cannot find its limits and tries to be something else. Then it pretends; shows small things to be great and reduces large things to small. Then it is mere display of words and not real creation. But when the poet is true, when he establishes the Infinite within the limits of the finite world, when he creates happiness within his power, then he is creative. His place is within all other created things in the world. The work that is produced by a true worker, the worshipper of truth who creates life , he has the right to be seated in line with others. Carlyle and other scholars who have given more emphasis on work than upon mere words clearly demonstrate that they have more faith in the establishment of truth than on false words. It has also to be admitted that true words are much more important than false deeds.

The fact is whichever way truth is expressed it is one and the same thing. It is man's permanent asset. When money is truth, or in other words, when strength expresses itself through money, in that case money is not merely money. It is food, clothes, education and health. Because that money's valuation is bound within the limits of truth, it can overcome its specific limitations. In other words, it gets united with different external elements of truth through its real worth. Similarly there is a link and comparability of true poetry with man's other aspirations of truth. True poetry does not remain confined within a few words in poetic form. It gets united with man's spirit, the work of people and the religious austerity of the ascetic. It is an undoubtable fact that if the world did not have poetry, then the various kinds of work by man would have been different. This is because man's true words always get mixed up with his true deeds providing him strength, shape and leading his path towards its aim.

Hence we have to remember this especially that getting to know truth within its limits is the only way to attain unlimited truth. If we exceed our own limits then we also overcome our own Infinity. In this world whenever man has been true, whether in poetry, or in deed or in religious pursuit, his difference from other ordinary men has been that he has been successful in discovering the limits of Infinity, while other have been wandering aimlessly without any definite aim. This vagueness is petty. When a river can access its own banks only then can it rush towards the ocean; but if it is dissatisfied with itself and tries to eliminate its banks with the desire to grow bigger, then its movement is stopped and it spreads itself in a petty lake or waterbody.

We have to remember that trying to limit oneself within the limits of truth is not narrowness, lethargy or effortlessness. In reality, man becomes liberal if he is placed on the throne of limitations; being arrested within the limits makes man's efforts more powerful. A person is recognized among human beings when he acts like a person; a nation can establish itself among other nations by claiming its nationality. That race of people who have not achieved nationality have lost their position among other nations of the world. The man who is great has realized himself more than others. The person who has found himself cannot remain stuck in inertness; he has found his work, his position, his happiness. He can move freely like a river, his own momentum makes him move, the limits of his truth guide him easily towards the true end.

Abirabirma Edhi, let He who is the glorified one express Himself in me, reveal Himself within my limits—this is the true prayer. If I neglect my limits then it shall cause an impediment to the revelation of that Infinity. *Pahi Mang Nityam,* O Lord, protect me always. Protect me within my limits, my truth, see that I do not lose myself outside those limits. Whatever I am, let me clearly realize myself as that and feel your happiness and pleasure within me. In other words, the way my limits are your pleasure, let me accept those limits with happiness and pleasure and make my own life successful; this is the fundamental innermost prayer of my existence.

London

[First published in *Tattwabodhini Patrika,*
Ashwin issue, 1319 B.S.]

Chapter 19

Limit and Infinity

The root meaning of dharma is something that holds. If we discuss the evolution of the word *religion* then we understand its meaning also to be something that bonds together.

So, in a way we can say that man has accepted religion to be a bonding. Religion has limited the area of man's efforts and constricted it. Man's greatest endeavour is to accept this bonding, to gain this limit.

This is because limit is creation. The more the boundaries of limitations are marked, the more true and beautiful creation becomes. The nature of happiness is such that it manifests these limits. God's happiness has encapsulated all creation within the limits of codes or laws. The worker, the poet, the artist are constantly creating more explicit limits within that happiness.

Religion is also the strength of man to enable his humanity bloom within the limits of truth. The more properly and clearly the limits are marked, the more well-defined it is, the more true and beautiful creation turns out to be. Man becomes healthier, stronger and more prosperous and his happiness becomes more expressive.

Man seeks both his limits and also the Infinite through religion. This is strange. We see this dichotomy in every complete thing in this world. That which demeans also uplifts, something that divides also unites at the same time, something that binds also releases. The Infinite creates the limits and this limit expresses the Infinite. In the literal sense, completeness occurs where this dichotomy blends into one whole. If it is divided and one side of the scale becomes tilted then it is inauspicious. When Infinity does not define the limits then there is emptiness; where the limits do not point out at Infinity, there it is useless. When freedom disclaims bonding then it is madness, where bonding does not acknowledge freedom there it is oppression. In our country the philosophy of maya defines all limits as illusion. But the truth is, the limit that is disjointed from the Infinite is illusion. It is also true that the Infinite that is detached from the limits is also illusory.

The song that has attained its complete limit not only expresses a collection of tunes but through its rules gives us joy and expresses something beyond its limits through those boundaries. The rose has completely blossomed within its limits and so through its limits radiates infinite beauty. Because of its limits this same rose is just another object in the natural world but it is the epitome of happiness in the world of imagination. This limit has bonded it at one side and let loose on the other.

That is why we see that behind all kinds of education is the need to practise restraint. Man can move when he can control his efforts, he can think when he can control his thoughts. That artisan who knows the limits of his work and who abides by the rules is highly efficient or competent. Only he who is controlled has been able to make his life beautiful. Just as a loyal wife restricts herself and therefore gets the full satisfaction of her love, so also in a similar way the man of clear conscience, someone who has bound his desires within the limits of truth, is able to obtain the ultimate fruit of his austere endeavour, his eternal happiness.

Religion has been accepted as a bonding and sorrow. It is said that the path towards religion is difficult to attain. If that path had spread wide then every human being would somehow have walked on it and no one would have any impediments towards the same. But that path is bound within definite limits and that is why it is difficult. Man has to accept as truth the sorrow of following his limitations. That is because it is through this sorrow that happiness is revealed. That is why it is stated in the Upanishads that He has created everything through the sorrow of the hard code of asceticism.

The poet Keats has said that truth is beauty and beauty truth. Truth is the limit, truth is the rule. Everything is realized through truth and the moment there is deviation from the truth or the limit, everything gets disturbed and is destroyed. The beauty of Infinity is expressed within the limits of this truth.

If we try to separate limitations and Infinity then the worship of religion by man becomes entirely fruitless. If

Infinity exists only outside limits then there is no bridge in the world through which it can be achieved. So for all of us He remains forever a falsehood.

But man's religion is telling him, 'If you attain your limits, you will attain Infinity. You attain your manhood and through that your worship of the eternal will be fulfilled.' Here is our fearlessness, our immortal nectar. We get our fulfilment from the truth that resides within our limits. That is why the Upanishads say—He is his ultimate movement, He is his ultimate wealth, He is his ultimate shelter, He is his ultimate happiness. Limitlessness and limits, He and him, are both very close to each other, like two birds sitting adjacent to each other.

The inner meaning of the religious principles in our country is that the bond between the limits and Infinity is a bond of love and happiness. This means that as limit is to limitlessness so limitlessness is to limit; one is naught without the other.

Man has sometimes pushed God off to some distant heaven and then that God had become terrible. In order to conquer that terrible God the fearful man has taken recourse to different kinds of prayers, rituals, priests and intermediaries. But when man came to know God intimately then his fear was destroyed and by removing the intermediary he tried to unite with Him through love.

Sometimes man criticizes and abuses his limits. Then he tries to torture his normal habits, leaves his society, and tries to attain the impossible through worshipping the

Infinite. He then thinks that the limits are his own, so even if he disgraces it no one else will be affected. But from where did man get this idea of limits? What does he know about the infinite mysteries of such limits? How dare he tries to cross the limits!

When man gets to know that the Infinite is to be found within the limits then he is able to understand that this mystery is the mystery of love; this theory is that of beauty and herein his glory lies. Also this glory is to man's God. Limit is the wealth of Infinity, its happiness, because He has given himself to us and accepted us through these limits.

London

[First published in *Tattwabodhini Patrika*, *Kartik* issue, 1319 B.S.]

Chapter 20

The Norms of Education

Before coming, I had made a resolution to go and view the schools here very closely—to see whether anything related to the system of education here could be utilized in our country. I have seen a few things by now and have read some of the discussions going on in the newspapers regarding the education system of the country. A lot of experiments are being done, and new methods of teaching are being invented. One group says that children's education should be made as joyous as possible; another group believes that without sufficient hardship during their school years they will not grow up as mature individuals later in life. One group says that the best way to be educated is to see, hear, feel and immerse oneself in nature and absorb everything from it; another group believes that the best results are obtained when one exerts one's power wholeheartedly and devotes oneself totally to learn all subjects. This debate will never be resolved because there is a duality in man's own nature; happiness teaches him, and so does sadness; he can neither do without discipline, nor can he esteem it without freedom. On the one hand he can seek things where they can be accessed freely; on the other, the road by which he can bring things through hard work and toil is also open for him. It is easy to ask people to identify the middle path and adopt it but it is practically impossible to make them follow it in practice. This is because life does not flow in straight lines. Due to various impediments and pressures both from within and without, it flows like a meandering river and does not move onwards as a straight dug-up canal would. Thus it not only has to attempt to keep the line straight but also has to constantly change its position. What seems like its middle path now might turn into the corner position at some other time; what is the main path for one race might be the middle path for another. For all sorts of inevitable reasons in the history of mankind there is sometimes war and sometimes peace; sometimes wealth overflows and sometimes it ebbs away. Sometimes man is excited about his own ability; at other times he is upset by his impotency. Given the nature of things, when man starts leaning on one side, then the best course of education for him is to pull as firmly as possible to the other direction. It is easy to select a steady course when a man is balanced in his outlook. If he has control over his own body and is hit on one side, then he will be able to sustain himself by instinctively veering to the other; but a drunkard will fall down at the slightest push and will not be able to get up afterwards. The method of bringing up children in Europe has been evolving on its own. The more Europeans are coming into contact with different forms of experiential knowledge, the more they have been transforming themselves.

Therefore, the path of education should be determined according to the direction in which the spirit moves. But since there are many routes to choose from and not everyone can see them all clearly, no particular person or group will be able to show the right path with certainty at any point of time. The correct path must ultimately be chosen through the collective effort of different people. This is why for all races, keeping open the route to self-examination is the only way to discover the truth.

However, in a country where even a hairline deviation from the societal framework of order and education is tantamount to losing one's caste, there is a huge impediment at the very root to civilizing oneself in such a country. No one can prevent the changes taking place in a society and changes will always take place in it. But there can be no bigger misfortune for humanity if people bind themselves permanently to set rules. Why is this so? When a river deviates from its original path, the concrete steps built on its embankment remain in the same place; the route for crossing the river on a ferry boat remains same; if the passengers alight at any other ghat than the one built for them, they will end up being ostracized by society. So there are ghats but no water; there are boats but no movement for them.

This is also why our society has not been giving us the education suitable for our time; it is still giving us the sort of education that is 2,000 or 4,000 years old. So the sort of comprehensive schooling that can make us good human beings is not available for us. The society makes no demands on our lifestyle that is at par with the modern times. When we look at the present age we realize that the form of education accessible to us is not relevant to our needs. Once upon a time the social structure had required some people to be Brahmins, some Kshatriyas and some Vaishyas or Shudras. It was a claim on us that was concurrent with the times. Keeping in mind this demand, the educational system had created itself in a unique manner. Because it is the law of creation; in order to live, the basic seed of a fundamental idea that has been planted, sprouts urged on by the need of life and then spreads its own branches and stems; its branches are not grafted from elsewhere. At present there is no dynamic claim of our society. Even now it is telling people, 'Be Brahmins, be Shudras.' But it is no longer possible to follow truthfully what they are preaching; hence a man accepts these dictums only superficially. There is no true austerity required of a Brahmin; nowadays just shaving the head and enacting some farcical acting for three days enables a person to wear the sacred thread. Now a Brahmin cannot teach lessons about the purity of life that he has learned about through austere practices, he is all too eager to bless people with the dust on his feet. On the one hand, the foundation of caste difference that is professional classification is no longer something that is practised or tenable; on the other, the external rules and regulations of caste distinctions have become totally redundant. We have to put up with the cage with all its iron bars and chains; although the bird inside is dead. We are regularly supplying food but it is not being consumed by any living being. This split between our lifestyle and our social mores has only resulted in useless traditional practices that are not only in conflict with the times and act as impediments but we are also unable to preserve truth in our social life. We pay a price and take in but in this transaction there is no genuine gain. The fact is that there is nothing genuine around us that can replace it. The disciple does obeisance to the guru and repays him; but the guru does not make the least bit of attempt to repay his credit to the disciple. Instead, he instructs his disciple in an ancient and forgotten language—the latter does not have the reverence needed to accept it, neither the capability nor the wish to do so. The net result is that we are gradually losing faith in the idea that truth is at all necessary for us. As long as we manage to keep up appearances we do not feel at all ashamed to state that we are happy with the way things are. We do not even hesitate to claim that as long as you do not concede publicly that you are guilty of misconduct, you can behave as badly as you want. Ninety-nine per cent of people in society won't hesitate to abide by such falsehood under duress because society still strictly binds with rigidity all conduct even when your intrinsic respect leads you to following a different path. Brave men are few in number, and when the punishment for admitting truth becomes intolerable, one can no longer consider falsehood as a crime. This is why we find this strange situation in our country where a man can easily admit something as good but also declare at the same time that he is unable to abide by it in social conduct. When we think that the penalty for implementing one's beliefs is so unreasonably great, we also decide to forgive such falsehood.

Thus, where in society it is no longer possible to direct the flow of life towards a healthy and balanced outlook, and where old customs prevent progress at every step there it is not as if such schools that are among the most natural and open for mankind is not there for us, things becomes even more dangerous for us because they exist and at the same time are not there in spirit. Instead of showing the way to truth, they tend to encourage falsity instead. Not wanting to recognize movement, this society defiles whatever is static in it.

And if such is the moribund condition of schools in society, consider the nature of the state-supported schools. That too is a structure that has been moulded carefully. Its only goal is to try and mould all the different methods of education into one fixed pattern. The idea that it fears most is that the country might develop its distinct method of doing things. Its main motive is to maintain sole control over the mind of the country and implement its own laws. Thus this huge educational mechanism is turning into a mechanism for producing clerks. People here are collecting notes and stuffing themselves with sackful of degrees, but that is not the way to nurture life. A man may be proud of carrying on his shoulders a big load of degrees, but may find no reason to take pride in the soul.

Both the old shackles of community schools and the new shackles of the state-supported schools have not been liberating our minds to the extent to which they are tying it. This is our only problem. I do not want to entertain the new methods through which memorizing history or solving mathematics has become pleasurable. I know that when we seek new methods we look for cheap but impossible ways. We tend to believe that since the right people are not available readily, we must try to fill up the deficiency by following the conventional path. Man has repeatedly attempted that path and repeatedly failed in the process, putting himself in trouble. However we might wander in search of new means, in the end we have to come back to the unavoidable truth that education is imparted by teachers, not by methods or rules. The mind of man is fluid and another fluid mind aids his understanding best. A few famous teachers have been born in our country since ancient times like the river Bhagirath, it is they who have attracted the pure stream of education and have reduced the burden of evil in society removing the stagnation of death. Even within the fixed norms of education they have been able to imbibe life in the minds of students. Just remember the beginnings of English education in our country. Derozio, Captain Richardson, David Hare—all of them were teachers and not carriers of bundles of notes. The walls of the university at that time were not made out of concrete to the extent that they are now. Light and wind could then enter through them freely; each teacher could then establish his own position within the space left by norms of those times.

The walls around the education system of our country have to be demolished at any cost. We are not getting results because we have been engrossing ourselves in political movements and other external paths that are dispersing our efforts. We ourselves have to shoulder the responsibility of imparting education in our country in an atmosphere of freedom by directing that strength and energy into the channel of success. This is the most important task for people who want to devote their lives to the welfare of our country. It is only when the stream of education is enlivened through the different experiments made by different teachers that it will acquire the natural entity of our country. Only then shall we be able to see the emergence of the teacher at different moments and at different places. Only then will a tradition of teaching be established in a natural manner. We cannot implement a special norm of education merely by labelling it as 'national'. The education that is being implemented by different people in our country through different ways and means only that may be called national. Whether directed by our own people or by foreigners, if one particular educational norm tries to impose itself on the nation as the only true one then it cannot be called national. On the contrary, it is a sectarian method and hence very harmful for the nation.

We had once learnt a great truth about education. We had learnt that man could only learn from another man. Just as only water can fill up a pond, a flame can only ignite fire, one spirit lights up another. If a man is mowed down, he cannot remain a man. He then becomes a tool required in offices and factories; he then wants to become a teacher instead of a human being; he will not then be able to inculcate the spirit but will merely impart lessons. It is through the complete relationship of a guru-disciple that a healthy education can move as naturally as the way blood flows in a living body. The real responsibility of rearing a child and educating him lies upon the parents. But because parents may not have the capability or opportunity to do so, it may become necessary to depend on a qualified person. It is then that a guru has to end up adopting the role of the parent. We cannot buy the best things in life with money or accept them in parts; we can only absorb them through love and respect. That is the juice that helps humans digest knowledge; that is what can help them to absorb inanimate objects. At present the exemplary figure of the guru has become the most essential element in our country's educational system. There is nothing more harmful in childhood than a lifeless system of education; it grinds the mind out and saps it instead of nurturing it. In our social system we are on the lookout for a guru who will bring dynamism to our lives; in our educational system we are looking for a guru who will remove all obstacles from the path of movement of our souls. At any cost, we need to build human beings everywhere; no *kaviraj* will be able to save us by making us swallow drugs consisting of methods instead.

Chalford

Sravana 31, 1319 B.S.

[First published in *Prabasi, Ashwin* issue 1319 B.S.]

Chapter 21

Aims and Education

One of my friends deals in the study of applied astrology. He once told me that those people who have nothing special, those who do not have any yes and no clearly demarcating their lives, astrology cannot correctly define them. It is very difficult to ascertain the effect of good planets and bad planets in their lives. A strong wind in the sail of the ship enables it to move very fast and cover two days of journey in one day. It does not take long to utter these words but we cannot predict whether the paper boat will move in a directionless manner, or sink, or what will happen to it. The past or the future hardly matters to those who do not have a particular port to call. What shall he wait for, what will he prepare himself for? In the hope-thermometer the highest limit of his inordinate ambitions is close to the despair level of other countries.

The present condition of society in our country is at its worst. We do not have clarity in our lives. Nowhere in our country is it mentioned in thick and bold lines what we can become or how much we can wish for. The right to wish actually enhances the strength in man. In nature's household there can be no wastage and so strength departs from where there is no hope. Science tells us that if creatures with eyes are confined inside a house for a long time then they gradually start losing their vision. Nature cannot tolerate the contradiction that there will be vision when there is no light. Similarly it is intolerable for nature that there will be strength without any hope. That is why when there is no way to run away from danger, the strength to run away is also lost.

That is why we see that if we expand our field of hope then man's strength also increases. Then strength can see the road clearly and so walks with bold footsteps. In any society the greatest gift that can be given to man is hope. Not that every man in society can get full success out of that hope; but because he progresses towards that hope both knowingly and unknowingly, it inspires each person to reach the utmost limits of his strength. This is the greatest thing for a nation. There is no value in the size of a population, but that of the total number of people most are trying to engage themselves in work that is rich in the strength quotient and are not buried under the earth—this is prosperity. Wherever power is in a state of motion, it is beneficial; wherever wealth is labouring out of liveliness, therein lies prosperity.

In this western country everyone has heard the call for achieving the target; everyone more or less knows what he wants; and that is why everyone has come prepared by fitting arrows in their own bows. Everyone has come prepared to shoot at the target hanging high above and be able to win the one born out of the sacrificial fire and known by the name of Yajnaseni or Draupadi. We have not been invited to this occasion of hitting at the bull's eye. Therefore there is no reason to think excessively about what to attain; it is unnecessary and it is also not clearly defined in front of us where we have to go.

That is why when I listen to this sort of questions, 'What will we learn? How will we learn? What are the different methods through which we can become educated?' then this idea comes in my mind—education or learning is not an artificial thing which has no connection with life. What we will become and what we will learn—both these things are adjacent to each other. However big the vessel is, it cannot hold more water than its capacity.

We do not have many things to demand. Society is not beckoning us for doing great work, nor drawing us for a great sacrifice. It does not require any explanation from us except for certain artificial meaningless routine matters like rising up and sitting down, eating, touching, etc. The royalty has also not opened up any wide space for movement in front of us; so whatever little hope we can expect within that thorny enclosure is essentially insignificant. Also, whatever little we can see through the holes in the fence is also very little.

Since we cannot see life in a greater expanse we do not think about it in a big way and naturally we do not even have it in our mind to aim for a higher goal and sacrifice our lives for it. Whatever little we think about it is entirely through textbook knowledge; whatever little work we do is just by imitating others. We have more trouble because those who open our cage for a moment, they go on repeatedly saying, 'You do not have the power to fly.' A fledgling does not learn to fly after graduating with a BA degree; it learns to fly because it gets the opportunity to do so. It sees everyone fly in its society so it knows for certain that it has to fly. The idea that it is possible to fly does not ever occur in its mind and make it weak. It is our misfortune that others constantly question our power and ability and because we do not find any space to prove that that suspicion is false, we keep on questioning ourselves and that disbelief about our own self gets rooted within us. This is how man loses faith in himself and he cannot even attempt to cross any big river; he hovers around near the shore in a very small space and remains completely satisfied with it and the day he somehow manages to go against the current from Baghbazar to Baranagar he feels that he has achieved a feat similar to that of Columbus.

What our country needs to educate people the most and to remind him day in and out is that he is bigger than a clerk, greater than a deputy magistrate. Like a firework whatever you are learning is not to somehow reach the sky of a school teacher's job and after that turn into ashes and fall on the ground like the bare skeleton of a pension holder. The education to recite this mantra silently is the most important education that can be imparted in our country. This is what we have to remember day and night. The stupidity of not understanding this is our greatest foolishness. Our society does not make us understand this, our schools also do not teach us this.

But if anybody thinks that I am frustrated with my country, then he will misunderstand me. We need to know clearly where we are located and in which direction we are moving. However unpleasant that knowledge is, it is the first and foremost requirement. Till now we have deluded our own selves about our misfortune and have tried to soothe ourselves somehow. It is no use saying that our traditional society is the best one in the world which helps us to grow up into a complete human being; such a strange exaggeration which is visibly being proved wrong in human history every day, to declare it with fanfare deliberately by force is an excuse for effortlessness. The person who never does anything or will not even move around will try to say these things and save himself from the criticism of others. We should do away with this illusion right at the beginning. When a doctor operates a boil then the wound always tries to cover up the mouth of the wound after surgery but a good surgeon ignores that effort of the boil. He leaves the mouth of the wound open every day till such time the signs of healing are clearly visible. The great boil of our country has got a great surgical treatment from the Almighty; this pain is her due; but every day she tries to evade and cover up the wound. In order to hide her insult as a falsehood she is trying to nurture that insult forever. But the more she tries to cover-up the wound, the surgical instrument of the doctor will break open that falsehood. It has to be admitted clearly one day that the boil is not an accidental manifestation that has been joined externally . It is an internal disease and the trouble is not external. The blood has become infected otherwise this terrible weakness, this hypnotic static state cannot keep man subdued in all matters for such a long period of time. Our own society has made our humanity diseased, has overpowered its intelligence and strength and that is why it is unable to cope up in society in any way. This forcible break-up of the false ideologies about oneself is not a sign of despair or effortlessness. It is the way to free the path of effort and break the nest of false hopes and do away with despair once and for all.

I want to state that in no country is education totally completed in school and it is also not so in our country. Digestive capability is not manufactured in the sweetmeat shop, only food is made there. Wherever man is greatly enthusiastic, there his education mixes with his nature. Because we cannot direct our life we cannot as well incorporate textbook knowledge within our hearts.

One might therefore think then where is hope for us. Because the path of life is not completely in our hands; the door to power can never be open for a subservient nation.

Though this is true, it is not the complete truth. In reality, the field of power is limited in some way or the other for people of all races. Everywhere the combination of both inner nature and external circumstances fixes up a person's own space. This well-defined space is essential for everybody because to disseminate power does not mean the utilization of power. In no country does favourable condition give man unlimited independence because that is failure. What our fate gives us is shared among us—those who get a bigger share of something on the one hand are bound to miss out something on the other.

So, it is not so important for man to realize what he has got; how to accept and utilize it is much more important. Whatever social or psychological circumstance prevents this ability to accept, paralyses that utilization power is the root cause of destruction. When man does not test anything before accepting it, always tells us to accept all small and big things through a set of fixed belief and fixed rules, however favourable the condition is, humanity is bound to be belittled. We keep on complaining about our limited capabilities, but we do not even know what our real condition is. We have not tested it from all quarters. That tendency to test it is considered sacrilegious and we have first and foremost tied it up with ropes. Because we do not have faith in human nature we tend to totally forget that if you do not allow man to make mistakes then man cannot be given scope for learning. If we do not encourage man and give him ample scope, belittle him in every which way through the rules of tradition and keep him forever imprisoned in the garb of goodness, no generosity of fortune can do any permanent obligation to them till they break up the shackles themselves and stop worshipping that shackle more than their hands and feet.

There can be no weakness as thinking that one's condition is more powerful than one's strength. If man can channel the force of this desires beyond personal interests, personal freedom, then there isn't any external condition in which he cannot grow up. In fact, that condition of external poverty helps him to grow up. In our country narrow bamboo posts are fixed around the sprout of the jackfruit tree to enable it to grow taller. That sapling therefore cannot spread out its branches all around. So it tries with all its strength to move towards light across the fencing of bamboo posts and with its fixed determination crosses its barrier. But this terrific force must be ingrained within the core of that sapling that, 'I must grow up. If I don't find any light beside me then I shall go upwards looking for it. If I don't get freedom in one direction then I shall not leave things unturned and try and gain it in another way.' If any living object states—'It's sinful to attempt anything—it's best to remain as I am' then that implies that for it the bamboo fence and the eternal sky are the same.

I firmly believe that man's most desired object can never remain unreachable. If the freedom of our race is not found around us then it is surely there upwards is something we can't forget for a single moment. We see the proliferation and growth of branches on all sides around us and that is why we consider it to be the greatest truth. But growing upwards is also a movement in life; there too we can gain the fruit of success. Actually speaking, whether on one side or another, we have to acknowledge the attraction of the Supreme Being; we will have to grow up and grow up further. We have to listen to such beckoning that draws us out from corners; that gives us readily the strength of self-sacrifice; that which does not keep our ambitions confined to the four walls of the office and our jobs. When that force is infused into our national lives, when that force will become mighty, then each moment we will overcome our present condition. Then no external drawback can make us feel ashamed in any way.

We cannot see present history in a well-defined manner, and that is why when light is approaching even then we fear the darkness to be eternal. But I clearly believe that a consciousness has struck our hearts. It will gradually exert its own force and never let us rest in peace. The exuberance of our heart will never die; it has to be kept alive in whichever way possible; it is that indomitable life force which is pushing us towards light through whichever opening it can. Man tends to forget that path which is forever open in front of him; the king cannot put up any impediments on that path and poverty cannot steal it too. I can clearly see that the path of righteousness is beckoning our mind and spirit that is hurt and checked everywhere towards liberation. In our country the call for treading this path is repeatedly heard from different corners through different voices. There is no such awakening in the world as this spiritual awakening; it makes the dumb speak, and the physically challenged climb over the mountain. It will awaken all our spirits, lead all our efforts; with the light of hope and happiness of music it will enliven and glorify our long-deprived lives. The more that ultimate goal of human life becomes clear in front of us, the more we can offer ourselves generously and all the petty webs of desire will be torm apart. If we consciously remember this aim of our country only then we can impart the education of our country the form of truth. Life has no meaning if there is only education but no goal. That our India will be a land of endeavour, a space for the austere worshipper, a place of karma for the sadhus, here will be lit the holy pyre of the highest self-sacrifice, if we nurture this glorious hope in our hearts, then the path will automatically be created and a pure education system will sprout, grow leaves and fruits.

Chalford, Gloucestershire
August 19, 1912
[First published in *Tattwabodhini Patrika*, *Agrahayan* issue, 1319 B.S.]

Chapter 22

Letter from America

Today is Sunday. The church bells are ringing. On opening my eyes in the morning I saw everything has turned white with snow. The black sloped roofs of the houses have opened their bosoms to the arrival of this all-encompassing whiteness and they are saying, 'Sit down on the darkness lightly!' Obliterating the realm of mud and dust-laden roads on which people walk, this stream of static whiteness seems to be moving along forcefully. There is not a single leaf on the trees; the top of the *Shukram Shuddham Papabiddham* (the bright, holy and pure) branches have received His blessings. The grass on both sides of the road are not yet covered completely like the last sign of youth, but are gradually bending their heads in defeat. The birds have stopped calling; there is no sound anywhere in the sky. The snow is flowing around and falling on the ground but its footsteps cannot be heard at all. The monsoon comes, resounding the earth and sky with the sound of the rain, the rustling of the leaves and branches, *Rajvadunnatadhwanih,* like the announcement of the arrival of a king—but while we were all asleep, the gateway of the sky had opened silently; no messenger arrived with its news, it did not wake anybody from their sleep. From the secluded hermitage of heaven, Silence is descending on the earth; it does not have the rolling sound of chariot wheels; Matli, the charioteer of Lord Indra is not controlling His wild horses with the reins of lightning and bringing Him to us; He is descending with His white wings spread out—His spread is soft and His movement unhindered. There is no collision anywhere; it does not hurt anyone a bit. The sun is covered; there is no fierceness in its rays; but the whole world is lit with a coy radiance—it is a brightness covered with peace and humility—its covering is its expression.

In this quiet winter morning I bow my head in obeisance to the arrival of this beautiful pure whiteness—I welcome it in my heart. I say –'You gradually cover up everything—all my thoughts, my imagination, cover up all my work. Covering up the darkness of midnight let your purity descend on my life silently, let it awaken my new dawn with pure whiteness—*Vishwani Duritani Parasuba*—let all faults be wiped away forever—do not keep any defects anywhere—just as the light from your heavens is perpetually pure so also cover up my life with unending whiteness.'

I am bathing my soul in the unending whiteness of this morning. It is too cold and difficult. I will have to bare myself naked like an infant and gradually sink into it so that nothing will be left behind—whiteness above, whiteness in the middle, whiteness in front, whiteness at the back, whiteness in the beginning, whiteness at the end—*Shiva eva Kevalam*—an all encompassing whiteness like Shiva. Sinking my entire body and mind absolutely in this whiteness I shall bow to the lord—*Namaha Shivaya cha Shivataraya cha*—who is benefactor and saviour and also to Him who is different.

I am watching how the appearance of old age can be so great, so deeply beautiful. All the diversities have been gradually and silently covered up; the unending whiteness has hidden behind it. All the songs have been covered, life has been covered, all the varieties of colours have got submerged in white. But this is not the shadow of death. What we know as death is black in colour; emptiness is not white as light; it is dark as a new moon night. The white rays of the sun have covered up all the red and blue rays; but instead of destroying, have completely absorbed it. Today the deep song of silence has filled up my soul. Today the trees and plants have all shed their covering; not a single leaf has been spared; it has absorbed all the wealth of life in the unseen depth of the heart. The goddess of the woods seems to have completed all her sermons and is only silently praying to herself with the Omkar mantra. It seems to me that the hermit Gouri has rejected all the jewellery of spring flowers and dressed up in pure white clothes is praying to the white image of Shiva. In this she is eroding both the desire that ignites passion and the desire that creates separation. All the evil of fiery passion is gradually diminishing; as far as we can see, everything is covered in white and there are no impediments for the union with Shiva. Now the wedding is approaching, the message is already written in the astral light of the Ursa Major, its secret preparations are going on at the heart of this austere worship, the songs of celebration have gathered there, the basket of flowers meant for the exchange of garlands is being filled up behind the eyes of the world. Welcome this worship, O my soul, bend myself low and quieten me—let the white peace cover you in layers and in the fixity of the unknown snatch all your efforts; let the angel of purity come once and do away with all the waste of this life from one end to the other; after that this quiet covering of worship will be lifted one day; covering all directions and the entire world, filling with the sweet song of happiness will arise the new awakening, new life, new celebration of union.

Agrahayan 9, 1319 B.S.
[First published in *Tattwabodhini Patrika,*
Falgun issue, 1319 B.S.]

Chapter 23

Letter from a Traveller to Vilayet

The ship is too crowded. Like the tide water of the river, the crowd that accumulates at the end of the market day is a moving crowd, but this crowd is a stagnant one. It seems we are in the clutches of a great giant and there is no way that we can escape from it. We, the first class passengers are in the clutches of his right hand. Those who have fallen in his left hand are more in number and there the pressure is more and space is less. Looking at the deck on that side it seems that portion of the ship is suffering from asthma—it cannot breathe sufficiently. We are in that phase of civilization which can be called the government age. It is a huge, complex and intertwined affair—be it railways, steamer, hotel, school and even mental asylum. Here the civilization states that the food allotted to it is the mass that is created after crushing the majority. It does not have sufficient space or capability to satisfy each person fully. This sort of governmental arrangement is gradually piling up every day both in the society and in the empire.

In this manner man's state and society has been built over enormous human killing. But I am sure a time will come when such people for sacrifice will no longer be easily available; when the whole group will demand its total value. Today the labourers are not obeying the dictates of the rich and powerful and for that reason society is annoyed. This means that the conglomerate power is bullying them and giving them the excuse of good state governance. They state that if you exceed your limits then the nation will suffer and other nations will prosper in spreading their business. But the labourers today are not wanting to listen to those excuses by saying that they will not tolerate injustice done against them; they deserve the full value of their work. In our country all this while we have demanded human sacrifice in the name of socialism; we have asked the Shudras—the untouchables—to give consent to their humiliation because that is the dictate of the collective god and that is their religion; we have told our women to agree to remain in prison for then they will be blessed by the collective god and they will maintain their dharma. But this collective god cannot compete with the eternal god and save us. The sorrow of demeaning human beings and doing wrong deeds is accumulating layer by layer both in state and society and in this manner it is nurturing the earthquake of destruction in its womb. The foundation of the state and society will be shaken, accounts will be demanded and then trying to repay this long-term debt, the conglomerate will be sold off or disseminated by the individual. Those who forcibly take away the individual's fulfilment and boast of collective achievement are under illusion because that success cannot last forever. Today we are trying to cover it up in the name of religion, but there have been many religions which have troubled our mother earth by baying at the blood of individuals for a while and tainted her with it but now they have completely disappeared.

I have been especially troubled with these thoughts for the past few days and let me tell you the reason for it. At the beginning of our voyage the passengers were complaining that the ship was moving rather slowly. The reason for this slow movement was that the people who had been assigned to shove coal into the fire in the engine, those helpless group of 'stokers', were new recruits and they were unable to function to the fullest extent. It was heard that in Bombay the dock labourers were to go on strike on a particular day. In order to avoid that, the stokers were promised extra money and made to work harder so that they could somehow reach the dock on time. One stoker with a shovel of coal in his hand fell down in front of the engine and he was killed due to fatigue and the unbearable heat. But the ship managed to reach before the strike commenced. There is no use in lamenting over such individual sorrow because we have to keep it in mind that we cannot get coal from the mines if we do not sacrifice a few lives; the ship doesn't cross the ocean and reach the port unless a few stokers are dead. Civilization requires collective wealth and that thought has to be kept alive above the sorrow of these people. All this is acceptable but we also have to remember that however happy we are, whatever advantages we might have, whether we call it civilization or something else, sorrow and injustice can never be covered up forever. The people who have been sacrificed are dead for now but later they will kill those who had tortured them. You must surely remember that Greece, Rome and Egypt died at the hands of those who were sacrificed and India is also being killed for a long time at the hands of people it has tortured. There can be no exception to this rule in history—our scriptures tell us that dharma or religion dies and then the same religion kills others. But that religion is not the shrewd one of the collective godhead; that dharma is the eternal religion of the gods.

May 19, 1920

We have crossed Aden and are now travelling through the Red Sea. Here we are crossing the sky of warm winds and entering the sky with cold winds. Different people from different parts of the world have divided and defined it by different names, but basically the real division is between the cold countries and the hot countries. According to this division the water and the wind of the earth are channelized to result in the formation of the cloud and the rain in the sky along with the different varieties of vegetation in different parts of the earth. Different forms and traditions of history are moving from one part of the world to another and they clash with each other and create a commotion in civilization. That too is the result of the power of opposite forces of this hot and cold weather. The inherent natural contradiction and variety of hot and cold will never be resolved. We belong to a warm country and we will do our work according to our thought patterns; they are people from the cold nations, and so they will think differently. We will sell our wares at their market and their products in ours, but it shall never happen that our fruits will be borne in their trees or their fruits in ours. The power with which the world is being ruled is the power of the cold air—that power is easy for Japan because she is in the cold air region but that is impossible for us. Every man can use a special power for a brief period of time, but if he does not get the favour of a suitable wind then it is impossible to keep control over that power or keep on maintaining or flourishing it. In the context of unending adversity of the gods there will gradually come lethargy and tiredness and then that will create distortion. It is very easy to understand this idea when we travel from one part of the world to another in a ship. The diversity of creation is readily discernible through your entire mind and body when we cross the Indian Ocean and come to the Mediterranean Sea. After listening to these words you might say, 'Do you then mean to say that we will have to completely surrender ourselves to the functions of external nature? Can't we overcome it by our sheer will force?' The answer to this is that we cannot say that you have to surrender, but special importance must be given to the effort. The entire civilization of man has been created by the confluence of external and mental phenomena; man can change this external phenomenon to a certain degree but that change is quite petty, it cannot be changed in its entirety. Then what is the function of our will power? The function is this—whatever we have attained we should make it entirely successful and not meaningless by sloth and inaction. Just as there is diversity in the circumstances, so also there is diversity in success.

I am travelling between two continents. On the left is Egypt and Arabia on the south. Both the shores are without human habitation and the bare gray mountains on both sides seem like jealous demon brothers who are eyeing one another with shrewd looks. And the depth of the ocean from which both of them have been born seems like a woeful mother standing between two fighting brothers and pleading with tearful eyes for them to remain separate from each other. The left shore is totally quiet, the right shore is also the same. But I am thinking of the drama that has been enacted by human history on both shores. The human civilization that had flourished in Egypt is ancient and wealthy. It has so many pictures, so many ceremonies, so many temples. And the sudden flourish that was seen in Arabia had so much of enterprise, enthusiasm and power. But the flourish of the human heart on both these shores was of totally different nature. Egypt established herself within her own huge organization and Arabia went on conquering one country after another with her indomitable force. The reason for the different nature of these two civilization was their geographical disparities. Fed by the River Nile, Egypt was fertile and full of vegetation and the people there were not suffering constantly from want or poverty. The deprived and undernourished sons of the Arabian desert were themselves disturbed and they went on disturbing everyone else in the world.

Just as Vasisthya and Viswamitra were two different sages with different personalities, so also Egypt and Arabia are two different classes of countries. All the people of the world can be divided into two broad categories and put in the Vasisthya and Viswamitra camps. Vasisthya resides in one place and Viswamitra moves around. Vasisthya tends to the cows and Viswamitra steals them. Vasisthya gives sermons in Ramchandra's ears and Viswamitra gives weapons in his hands. Vasisthya is the priest of a rich household and Viswamitra is the leader of a wild path.

At the present age India and China are the disciples of Vasisthya and Europe is restless at Viswamitra's beckoning. Will these sages ever get together out of love? And if they can come together then will all the rivalry of the world come to an end? If you hope that peace will be reinstated on earth on that day when one of these two sages will die, then your hope will not be fulfilled because in this world both Vaisthya and Viswamitra are eternal. I have the belief that one day both these sages will perform a sacrifice where both sermons and weapons, the eternal nectar as well all utilities will blend together and the fire of that sacrificial fire will never be extinguished. If Asia and Europe can come and meet under one truth then man's worship will be fulfilled, otherwise his worship will repeatedly be marred by bloodshed.

May 24, 1920

[This letter was excluded from the collection of essays reflecting the poet's thoughts on travelling and life in the West called *Paschatya Bhraman*. But it was a part of the revised 1939 edition of *Pather Sonchoy* where Tagore rewrote this in colloquial language as 'Bichitra'. This was published in *Santiniketan (Asharh issue,*1327 B.S.) under the title 'Bilat-Jatrir Patra'.]

Chapter 24

Seven Letters

I

New York
Kartik 13, 1319 B.S.

With due respect and humility,

When the gods and the demons got down together to churn the ocean, then the great ocean had to give up everything that it contained in its belly. I don't know whether it ever made Vedavyas, the author of the Mahabharata understand how tormented it felt during that period. But it made this present poet understand very clearly. My stomach is not as huge as that of the ocean and it did not have any precious object in it, but the amount of suffering does not depend on the area or volume. That is why while crossing the Atlantic I could feel its unlimited sadness quite soon. It did not take long to realize that we are petty mortal beings located on land. Now I only feel that I will not see those dark waters, will not cross the ocean—however loud the horn of the steamer blows, I do not feel like leaving the shores. After landing on the shore the body is still very tired. Being rocked day and night it seems that my heart is turning loosely within the frame of my body. The ocean seemed to consider me as its rattle—it shook me with both its hands. It thought that it would create a confusion within my stomach by mixing up different kinds of rhythms, but after churning when it did not find any clue to fix the rhythms then the great ocean let me go as a sigh of relief.

The house at Surul has been acquired.

To Jagadananda Roy
[Published in *Visva-Bharati Patrika*,
Magh-Chaitra issue, 1376 B.S.]

II

508 High Street,
Urbana, Illinois
Kartik 23, 1319 B.S.

With due humility and greetings,
We have settled down in Illinois. The house is quite small, neat and clean, quiet and secluded. We cannot get any servants here—those who do the housework for us are known as help. They are not servants—a lot of boys and girls from respectable families do this work to earn a

living. Most of the housewives here have to work extremely hard—cook, clean, wash utensils, wash clothes, etc. When compared to the same standard of women in our country we find that they do not do even one-fourth of such work that the class of people who do this sort of work here. Besides that here they have other considerations too. They cannot spend their entire day in doing housework in a lackadaisical manner. Above that they study, listen to speeches, deliver lectures, entertain guests and keep oneself neat and tidy at all times. Also they take a considerable amount of responsibility to teach their children. Here there isn't a single servant in Professor Seymour's house. Both husband and wife share all the domestic chores among themselves—on top of that Mrs. Seymour has taken the responsibility to teach English daily to daughter-in-law. I do not understand how someone who has to work so hard manages to undergo this unnecessary responsibility just for the sake of loving Rathi. Daughter-in-law has taken the responsibility of doing some petty household work for us—till today we could not arrange for a help. She cooks, sweeps, makes the beds and Rathi too joins her in these works whenever he has time. Bankim and Somendra are staying with us.

To Jagadananda Roy

[Published in *Visva-Bharati Patrika*,

Magh-Chaitra issue, 1376 B.S.]

III

508, High Street,
Urbana, Illinois, M.A.

Dearest,

Since the time we have come here I have spent the time in Professor Brooks' house and Rathi and daughter-in-law have been guests at the Seymours'. Yesterday we could enter our own house. You know the manner in which people live their lives here. So we too have begun to live our lives in that American manner. This means there are no servants or cooks in the house, our mistress of the house is undertaking everything. Daughter-in-law cooks and cleans. Bankim is helping her a little and in lieu of that he gets free food and boarding. Of course this is possible because we have all sorts of facilities here. Here almost 75 per cent of the work can be done by pushing various buttons on the wall. Rathi has joined college here—his professors are very happy to teach him—everyone has also liked daughter-in-law. I have settled down here quite comfortably. There is no chaos anywhere—the sky is open, there is unlimited light and infinite leisure. Sometimes I totally forget that I have come to America—it seems as if I am in India. I am thinking that for some time I will take leave from all sorts of writing and only read plenty of books. I cannot express to you the beauty of the peaceful morning that is peeping through this window in front of me.

It reminds me of any dew-washed *Pous* morning back home. I am really loving it.

To Santoshchandra Majumdar, *Ashwin* 9, 1319 B.S.
[Published in *Prabasi, Ashwin* issue, 1341 B.S.]

IV

21 Cromwell Road,
South Kensington, S.W.

My dear Santosh,
I did not receive any letters from you in the last three/four mails so I didn't write to you. I know that you all are receiving my letters in someone or the other's name. By the time this letter of mine reaches Santiniketan then the gardens there will be full of the scent of shiuli flowers and in this golden autumn the sunrise and sunset will create a wonderful beauty amid the lotus ponds. Since I am being deprived of that well-known joy, in my mind I am exaggerating it against the beauty of the sky here. My mind says that there is no beauty in the sky here; it doesn't know how to make man forget many things. It is supposed to be a moonlit night now but that can be realized only in the almanac. There are definitely stars in the sky because we get descriptions of it in astronomy and there is no reason to doubt that there are clouds too. The sky here remains very genteel by wearing a black frock coat and a black chimney-pot hat and that is why it does not prevent people

from doing their work. The sky in our country makes us forget our work. The golden light of autumn mars all office work—the way the sky has always kept all its doors and windows open makes it impossible for the mind not to respond to its invitation. That is why in our Vaishnava poetry the flute that plays makes the housewife forget her household chores—it brings us out from all good and evil.

Our skies are for holidays, the sky here is for the offices. In their sky the bell chimes, in our sky the flute plays. This is why they call it struggle for life and we call it *jibalila*—the play of life. The different perspectives of God's beauty are hidden here. That is why they try to say that He is struggling to regain himself here. There is no rest in between. We have seen that rest, seen that beauty, heard the tune of that flute. But when that flute lures us, it brings us through a path which we tend to avoid because it crosses a different terrain. This is where we have been totally fooled. It is not enough to just listen to the music of the flute; we have to walk according to the tune of the flute and that is where we have to pass through sorrow. Thorns will prick the feet, but if you cannot tolerate it then how will the tune of the flute enter your heart? Till today happiness has come only through the path of sorrow—there are no other means. What is alluring us from the comfort of our bed is not the summons of an administrator but the tune of the flute.

Ashwin 9, 1319 B.S.

[Published in *Prabasi*, *Ashwin* issue, 1341 B.S.]

V

London

My dear Ajit,

I do not wish to spend the winter here. But on the whole the autumn has behaved decently—it seems that the tipsy way in which the sky behaved throughout the entire summer, it is now beginning to express its regret. We could enjoy sunlight for the last two weeks of September. Again for the last couple of days we were scared because the sky was filled with clouds. But the sun is shining brightly this morning. There is no dearth of sunlight in our country but even till this day I have not got over this thirst for sunlight. My mind gets overwhelmed on the day there is sunlight here. I feel like going to some far-off seaside place in the land of light and build a house there. Behind me will be the sea beach skirted with deep forests, in front, next to the quiet white sands the blue water will constantly move with the surf, on the west coast there will be mountains as if the earth is aimlessly attempting to reach the sky and a river will meander and come and fall into the ocean. The albatross will fly in the sky, the fishermen's boats sail over the blue water with their white sails spread out—and there will be a wide expanse of light over all these scenarios; all these sights fill my imagination and the deep vessel of leisure overflows with a golden light with the lyre in my heart playing at an equal pace. Like the tide of the river my time flows gradually into the ocean and no one wants an account of it. God has created man as a slow-moving creature—he cannot run like a horse, fly like a bird, there are many obstacles in his route of escape—that is why he has put in so much of speed and movement in the mind of man. Otherwise in such a morning who could have held me back?

To Ajit Kumar Chakravarty, *Ashwin* 16, 1319 B.S.
[Published in *Prabasi, Kartik* issue, 1341 B.S.]

VI

508, High Street,
Urbana, Illinois, USA

My dear Ajit,
I had a lot of hope that after reaching here I will just bask quietly in the sun the whole day and spread out my mind in the open blue sky. See, this complete laziness is my habit—within all my work I keep alive the hope of this bright, peaceful and deep vacation. I put my hands in my pockets and think that I have already purchased my weekend ticket—I will just board the train once it is Saturday. But unfortunately for me that Saturday never arrives—I can see that my week does not comprise of seven days; how many days it is exactly is also not clearly mentioned in my

almanac. No one else possesses such a runaway mind as I do. When I was young I ran away from school, even when I grew up, nothing could hold me back; I would jump up on the wall and run away. Even now I feel extremely tempted to run away from my own work. This kind of a clash of consciousness within oneself is seen only among very few people. All this while I have gone on knitting one work after another—but just as fish cannot live without water, similarly for me it is the wide unlimited expanse of the sky—I get habitually very upset if I don't savour it. After coming here I have become too much involved with work. In London I was engrossed with my art of poetry, here it is prose. I probably wrote to you earlier that I delivered a lecture on Universalism in the local Unitarian Church and that did not cause me much sorrow because a lot of it was translated by Satishbabu and I expanded and altered sections of it to make it presentable. For the second time I had to write the entire thing myself. That was good. The subject was self-reliance. It was not the translated version of the existing Bengali lecture—I wrote a new piece on the same topic. The professors here liked it. There are a couple of Germans here who have shown a lot of enthusiasm. There is a physics professor here called Kunz who is popular in this country as an expert in his field. After my lecture on that day I had a long discussion with him till late at night. His enthusiasm has enthused me. This week I have written another article on the topic of worshipping the Brahma—I will read that tomorrow and I am also preparing to write another lecture for the following week. I cannot think right now when and how it will stop. It seems I have created another whirlpool and this will toss me around in America for some time. I have no more holidays, but my mind wants holidays. Till now I don't understand which mind of mine works and which mind only looks for holidays. I had run away from school and that was a pretty easy task; but it is not so easy to escape from the trap set by yourself. I keep on thinking—the butterfly once wraps itself up in its net of millions of threads and again when time comes the same butterfly comes out of its net on its own. My turn will also come one day. Then I will not draw these fine lines of pen and ink around my leisure hours. I will then do something even if I don't do anything and will speak even if I don't say anything.

To Ajit Kumar Chakravarty, *Agrahayan* 8, 1319 B.S.
[Published in *Prabasi, Jaisthya* issue, 1342 B.S.]

VII

508 High Street,
Urbana, Illinois

With due respect and greetings,
Jagadananda,
All these days we have been enjoying almost unending sunshine here. People here usually do not get to see such

a pleasant view of nature in the months of November and December. It has started raining from the second or third day of January. That day a spell of snow fell and turned everything white, after that it rained heavily for the rest of the night, exactly like the monsoon rain in our country. In the morning I saw that the same rain had frozen on the streets, on tree tops, on telephone wires, to become snow. The road has become extremely slippery—Somendra has slipped and fallen down once or twice almost every day—and later at night it rained once again. The next day the layer of snow became thicker and harder. The trees seemed to be covered entirely with glass, the branches breaking and falling down with the weight of the snow and making a lot of noise. A tree fell down over the electric wire and so all lights were off at night. There are very few pedestrians on the streets with almost no cars boasting around. For a couple of days I did not go out at all. If you slip and fall down at a young age then the loss is compensated but at my age that is supposed to be terrible—that is why whenever I find a possibility of slipping down, I feel it is sensible for me to sit at home. I have sat down and translated many poems. The sun has risen today. What a wonderful sight it is. The leafless branches of the winter trees are all shining like diamonds—it seems as if a series of crystal chandeliers have been fixed in the house of festivities. Yesterday the streets were as clear as mirrors—the snowfall at night has turned everything white. Today I wish to go out after I finish composing the letters. There is a complete possibility of falling down, but according to the worshippers of Shakti, even if you fall down you must rise up once again because the tricks of the snow are also visible here.

To Jagadananda Roy, *Pous* 24, 1319 B.S.
[Published in *Visva-Bharati Patrika, Magh-Chaitra* issue, 1376 B.S.]

Acknowledgments

Some of these essays have been published earlier in the following books and journals:

'The City of Bombay', 'Crossing the Ocean', 'Stopford Brooke' and 'The English Village and the Clergy' in *The Essential Tagore*. Eds. Fakrul Alam and Radha Chakravarty. Cambridge: Harvard University Press and Kolkata: Visva-Bharati Publications Department, 2011.

'In London' and 'The Norms of Education' in *Apperception: Journal of the Department of English and Other Modern European Languages*, Special Issue on Rabindranath Tagore, Visva-Bharati Vol. 7 (July 2014).

'Letter from America' in *Seminar 623*, Special Issue on 'The Nation and its Poet: A Symposium on Rabindranath Tagore 1861-1941: Life, Language, Legacy' (July 2011):89-92.

'Crossing the Ocean' and 'In London' in *Wanderlust: Travels of the Tagore Family.* Translated and edited by Somdatta Mandal. Kolkata: Visva-Bharati Publications Department, 2014.

About the Translator/Editor

Dr Somdatta Mandal is Professor of English at the Department of English and Other Modern European Languages, Visva-Bharati, Santiniketan. Having a teaching career that spans 32 years, she has held several administrative posts in the university including her current one as Head of the Department of English and Other Modern European Languages. Paper-setter, examiner and adjudicator for doctoral dissertations across several universities in India and the SAARC nations, she has lectured widely in national and international fora.

A recipient of several prestigious international fellowships and awards from the Fulbright Foundation, Charles Wallace Trust, Rockefeller Foundation, Shastri Indo-Canadian Institute and Sahitya Akademi, her areas of interest are American literature, contemporary fiction, film and culture studies, diaspora studies and translation. Published widely both nationally and internationally, she has published three books, five volumes of translation, edited and co-edited 22 books, published above 90 research articles in national and international journals and anthologies. She also has over 110 book reviews to her credit.

Dr Somdatta Mandal has published translations of several travel narratives, among which are Krishnabhabini Das's *A Bengali Lady in England* (2015); *Wanderlust: Travels of the Tagore Family* (2014), a compilation of the travel experiences of the members of the Tagore family as recorded in diaries and memoirs by them; Durgabati Ghose's *The Westward Traveller* (2010) and Hariprabha Takeda's *The Journey of a Bengali Lady to Japan and Other Essays* (in press). She has also edited two volumes of travel essays, *Indian Travel Narratives* (2010) and *Journeys: Indian Travel Writing* (2013). Her recent translation of Sukumari Bhattacharya's *The Comparative Popularity of the Ramayana and the Mahabharata* is in the press(Anustoop).She is presently translating Tagore's *Pathe O Pather Prantare.*